Theatre of Life

The Memoirs of Albert Edward Johns

From Merchant Navy Gunner to Pantomime Dame

By Albert Johns

(with contributions from Graham, Murray and Steve Johns)

ISBN 978-1-081-00805-5

This book is dedicated to Albert & Ethel, Mum & Dad, Grandpa & Grandma, publishing Albert's words by way of a small legacy of an interesting life.

It is also dedicated to those, on all sides, who lost their lives during the Second World War.

A PERSONAL NOTE

Thank you for choosing to read this memoir of Albert Edward Johns, my Grandpa.

On a purely personal basis, we (my Dad, brother and I) hope that you will take something memorable from it as a personal account of a life lived at times in extraordinary circumstances, from humble beginnings to the theatre of war and finally to the theatre of entertainment.

Since the idea of putting his words into print was first mentioned, it has been followed up with an interest which has been a great trip down memory lane for the family, reflecting on the fond things we remember about Albert; and a realisation that maybe there are more questions than answers. Thank you to all, either for sharing memories or in originally encouraging Albert to document his experiences and typing them up on his behalf.

Please bear in mind that this text is, in the main, the memories of an individual. We have done our best to verify timelines and names, and to correct any noted inconsistencies but due to our own timeline now being over fifteen years since Albert's death, it is sadly not possible to go back to him to double-check the facts presented. That said, I would like to offer thanks for the assistance from www.maritimearchives.co.uk in verifying some of the details within. Thank you also to the Nottingham Post for their permission to reproduce archive newspaper articles.

Reviews are so important for self-published works to get noticed so, once you've reached the end, do please take just a few minutes and post an honest and constructive review on Amazon or Goodreads.

Graham Johns, 2019.

FOREWORD

BY THE JOHNS FAMILY

Some people may ask what is so special about a man from a humble, working class background that warrants this biography. In reality there's not too much other than he, effectively assisted by his wife, Ethel, chronicled events throughout his life. Many people living through those times did not get the opportunity to do so.

The period during the Second World War is of particular interest as it gives graphic details of life on the front line in the Merchant Navy, and the hostilities in the Mediterranean and North Atlantic. Albert's life in the theatre features after this, definitely the love of his life after his wife and family.

Before the onset of dementia, Albert said to his son, Murray, and his wife, Marjorie, that he would not have changed anything if he was to live his life again. We would actually question that and say there was possibly one thing he would have changed but we will come on to that later.

Albert's early life is covered in the first section of his memoirs. He was born the son of a Nottinghamshire miner and, in addition to his two elder sisters and three other brothers, we know there were other potential siblings who died at, or prior to, birth which was not an unusual occurrence in the early 1900s. Albert mentions a brother named Bill in his Early Years narrative, although Bill mysteriously disappears during one of the newspaper articles from the Second World War – and Murray can never recall Albert mentioning an older brother – it would be wrong to speculate on what happened to him.

Life was certainly tough in the early years and, quite often, his father would return home on payday with no money in his pocket, the local hostelries en route from the "Top Pit" in Hucknall being too big an attraction. As a consequence, Albert, along with his sisters, did much to ensure that their mother had money to feed the family, raising it wherever, and in whatever way, they could. Their entrepreneurial projects are covered extensively and many of them are quite amusing.

Albert's mother was right-handed and he knew that, if food was somewhat short, he stood more chance of a substantial meal if he got as close to her right as possible. It was common practice for her to serve the child on her immediate right first. There was, of course, always the chance of seconds on the rare occasions when food was plentiful!

His upbringing certainly did him no harm. He and his sisters all lived to their late eighties and it taught him to be resilient, respectful, supportive, loyal and faithful to both family and friends. Throughout his life, however, he seldom took risks.

His first regular job on leaving school was to work in Hucknall Main Colliery, the same place as his father and his brothers. He hated it, and his priority was to get out as soon as possible which was the cause of considerable conflict within the family group. Was the traditional family lifestyle not good enough for Albert? It certainly proved to be acrimonious at the time.

He achieved his move very quickly and went to work in the booming textile Industry at Bairnswear, a company manufacturing, as the name suggests, children's knitwear. This company played an important part in his life, as a place of work and a place to socialise.

The company, like so many from the 1960s onwards, was swallowed up by a major conglomerate, in the case of Bairnswear it was by Courtaulds. The changes they implemented proved to be unsettling and, after 38 years of service, Albert announced he was leaving to join Johnson & Barnes in Stapleford, where he was in charge of coordinating the distribution of yarn throughout the factory, amongst other things.

Can you imagine the family's surprise when he broke the news? Was Albert really serious? What about the risk of leaving the security of something he knew and was so convenient to home (he only lived 600 yards from the factory)? Basically he'd had enough and, with many of his former colleagues having moved to his new workplace, the wrench and uncertainty was less of a problem.

When he took early retirement from Johnson & Barnes he had only had three jobs throughout his career.

Ethel was a friend of Albert's sister Annie. After a brief courtship, they married on 9 June 1941 and they joked about him being the original toy boy as she was almost nine years older than he was. Ethel was born on 28 November 1907 in Wingham, Ontario (Canada) and many of the doubters said it wouldn't last. How wrong they were as when she died on 12 May 1994 they had been married for 52 years.

Like many couples of that time, their relationship was interrupted by the Second World War and Albert joined the Royal Navy. One day they asked for volunteers to work on the Merchant Fleet - everyone knows you never volunteer for anything in the forces and Albert swore blind he never did, the others must have stepped quickly back! From that day he was a gunner on merchant ships.

His memoirs contain graphic illustration of his wartime exploits plus those of his childhood. Albert was a good letter writer and Ethel carefully chronicled everything back in England. His exploits in the North Atlantic and North Africa make interesting reading and contain both sad and amusing moments.

We are sure his religious faith played an important part in his survival as he was torpedoed multiple times. On one occasion he had just been picked up from a lifeboat, changed clothes, had a hot meal and minimal rest, only to be torpedoed again.

Whilst on the North Atlantic run he made many friends on the Eastern Seaboard of Canada. People in New Brunswick welcomed the British into their homes and Albert remained in contact with many of these people. Sadly only one of them remains alive today and Lois Lutton greatly values Albert's friendship of 61 years.

In later years, due to Albert's failing health, Murray and Marjorie have maintained the friendship with Lois and visited her in 2004 when they saw many of the places in Canada which Albert fondly spoke of. This visit coincided with her 80th Birthday and, at the time of writing, she is now 94 years young.

Albert and Ethel visited Lois in 1972 and she was a welcome visitor to their home in 1979. In 61 years they only met twice, but their friendship was maintained and letters are still looked forward to by Murray and Marjorie.

With the War over it was time to resume normal service and Albert was able to pursue his passion for the stage. Along with other interested parties, they founded the Bairnswear Players and quickly established themselves as a very reputable amateur dramatic society performing from the stage in the works canteen.

They commenced with seasons of dramas and comedies, adding an annual pantomime to the calendar of events. Although Albert was an excellent straight actor it is his repeated role as Pantomime Dame for which he is best remembered locally. He brought happiness to many people but it sadly curtailed his involvement in dramas because everyone expected him to be funny. Albert Johns committing a murder, surely not?

So many people said he would have been a roaring success on the professional stage but he never took the gamble and this, we believe, was his one major regret. Those of us who saw him knew he would have succeeded as he had an inbuilt gift and talent which is lacking in so many entertainers.

Albert's solicitor, John Gamer, was another long-time friend of his from those early pantomimes and we can fondly remember John's silky skills on the drums as he performed in the theatre company's orchestra. Many of the family's friends were from the theatre as it was such an important part of Albert's life.

So, the "big stage" never materialised for Albert but the Bairnswear Players did take their shows to the Co-Operative Arts Theatre in Nottingham, a much larger forum than the converted canteen area at Bairnswear. They performed to sell-out audiences and the reputation of everyone involved with the group, including Albert, continued to flourish.

Unfortunately age takes its toll and Albert subsequently had to withdraw from the rigours demanded of a Pantomime Dame. He kept his hand in with small parts in shows at the Arts Theatre but, with Ethel's ill-health in the late 1980s, his involvement was sadly brought to an end. He greatly missed the theatre but his friends always made him welcome following his "retirement from active service".

Sadly, following Ethel's death in 1994 and this lack of involvement in theatre life, Albert's health did deteriorate. He decided to move into residential care, initially at Sycamore House in Sherwood. As his dementia became increasingly worse, it was necessary to move him into more secure accommodation. The last few months of his life were spent at Eden Lodge in Bestwood Village, where he was given excellent care and attention. It's unfortunate that his carers were not able to share some lighter moments with him because we know that they and the other residents would have enjoyed his humour and company.

Albert's quality of life was ultimately poor at his death, he was very reliant on carers so we're pleased he is reunited with Ethel once again.

The Johns family has never been what you would call a close family. Albert's sisters lived away and, from 1967 onwards, Murray seldom lived in the Nottingham area. The same situation exists today with Murray living in Spain, whilst Graham, Albert's eldest grandson, lives in New Zealand and Steve, Albert's youngest grandson, in South Yorkshire. The family has always lived a considerable distance from each other.

Not being near to each other does not diminish the concern, interest and love you have for your family. Albert was always interested in his family's careers and general well-being and the potential pitfalls of changing jobs.

He was an excellent father and he always had his family's best interests at heart. Sadly, because of his failing health, he was unable to share in their successes.

Even at his death, Albert's timing was perfect. He knew how to stage an exit. He died on 26 March 2004, the day after his 88th birthday, but on this occasion there was to be no encore.

ACT ONE – THE EARLY YEARS – 1916-1941

BY ALBERT JOHNS, EDITED BY MURRAY & GRAHAM JOHNS

"When I consider how my life is spent, Ere half my days in this dark world and wide…"

So wrote the poet John Milton, "On His Blindness"

This was a poem I learned as a child and, at the time, it impressed me very much. It now moves me to stop, think and ask myself in these, my twilight years, just how my life has been spent. Rewarding? … sometimes. Successful? … to a point. Interesting? … I would certainly like to think so. Exciting? … yes, and hair raising at times! Happily? … not always. Anyway, read for yourself and see what you think.

It was 25 March 1916 when I entered this world. The precise time I do not know but that was not important. I had arrived a perfectly healthy boy, the fourth child, and the second son, of Gilbert and Nellie Johns of 121 Annesley Road, Hucknall in the County of Nottinghamshire. Outside a blizzard was raging (so Mother told me when I was able to understand) although spring had been ushered in four days before. There's nothing unusual about that you may say, and I agree when you look at our weather patterns today. Sometimes we do not seem to know summer from winter!

From the very first moment the midwife slapped my backside, and I uttered my first cry, I seemed to sense that I had just been born into a very troubled world.

Born of humble parents in an era of war, want and deprivation, these factors have stood me in good stead and helped to mould my character. I am one who appreciates the simple things in life, one who has always been eternally grateful for small mercies. Blessed with an excellent memory, I can recall many detailed passages in my life and, strange enough, the more I remember, the more they seem to follow on and flood in, in quick succession.

Albert with his parents, Gilbert and Nellie, and Albert's dog

I don't recall my baby in arms and nappy days. No, I'm not as clever as that. Mother often related incidents which happened in those early months. Dad was in the War Hospital in London when I was born, having been injured on active service. Mother's chances of going to see him down there were nil as she could never have afforded it but good fortune smiled on them both when Eva Moore, the celebrated actress, paid a visit to the hospital. She asked Dad if he had relatives whom he would like to see if she sent for them and, naturally, he said he had a wife and newborn baby he had not seen. As a consequence of this, arrangements were made for us to visit, all expenses paid.

We stayed with Eva Moore at her London home and it was, to say the least, an education for Mother. She spoke of the lovely rooms, the beautiful wardrobes full of fabulous dresses and shoes and, of course, the hospitality shown to her by her host. Eva Moore was Jill Desmond's mother, who was Laurence Olivier's first wife.

Having spent over forty years in amateur show business myself, I had to laugh when my mother used to say, in all sincerity, "*I wonder if that's where you first got your taste for the stage?*" I'd like to think so, but I doubt it! Anyway, more about that later.

Whilst on the subject of casual remarks made by our parents which always gave us food for thought and came to fruition years later, I must tell you this: I was born with two crowns on my scalp and Dad always used to say "*Two crowns eh! That's a sure sign you will go across the sea before you die*". After five years in the Royal Navy during the Second World War I had done exactly that, time and time again! More of that later too.

Large families seemed to be the fashion in those days. Dad had four brothers and two sisters and, as if keeping up a tradition, he followed suit with a large family of his own. We boys were all named after our relatives – Bill, Walter, Harry and Albert – but my sisters had names of their own – Annie Elizabeth and Mabel Irene. To complicate matters even more on the subject of names, Mabel Irene was called "*Bessie*"! I think Grandma had called her that at some stage and it had stuck, but it certainly fooled many people who thought we had a bigger family than we really had, heaven forbid!

Dad was Head Ostler at Linby Colliery and worked underground for seven days a week for two pounds, eight shillings and one penny to keep his family. He loved his ale and the related pub life, and had to pass the Fox and Hounds and Portland on his way home so it was obvious that poor Mother got to see very little of his weekly income for housekeeping. His brothers had done much better for themselves and had good, responsible jobs elsewhere so we were looked upon as the poor relations. We were always known as "*Gilbert's kids*" by our patronising relations. How I used to loathe it when they called to give us Christmas gifts – there was a real Dickensian atmosphere in the old homestead.

I can honestly say that Dad, despite his faults, was a worker, or "*a grafter*" as he used to say. He never had a day off and he looked after the pit ponies as if they were his own. He was, however, always pleased when the pit closed for the summer vacation and the ponies were brought up from the mine to graze in a nearby field. We used to go with him everyday to see if they were all okay.

Bread, lard and pork dripping was part of the staple diet in those days, and good it was too, but have you ever had a slice that has been down the mine in a snap tin? It had a very different flavour and was so much tastier which I sense has come as a surprise to some of you. We eagerly awaited his coming home with a slice he may have left!

I knew very little of Mother's background except that she came from Bilton in Staffordshire and had a twin sister (Olive) and a brother (Steve). Her Dad, our Granddad who we saw little of, lived at 39 Steelhouse Lane in Wolverhampton and I got the impression their childhood days had been no bed of roses, but they never dwelt on the matter.

Mother had a dreadful inferiority complex, possibly because of this. She was very, very humble and did her best to please everyone and avoid possible confrontation. She was a fine mother in every sense of the word and, despite our living conditions, kept us well fed and respectable. We were poor but proud and our home was clean and humble with the soft soap and scrubbing brushes always in action. We always had clean window sills and the front door steps and pavement were always swept and swilled. It has to be said that this was a feature of life in this area.

Mother had an ever empty, concertina purse with many partitions in it but there never seemed to be anything in them. It was not because she did not work hard to try and fill it, on the contrary, it was washday every other day at our house as she took in washing and ironing to help swell the family income. Not an easy task when the weather was bad and it had to be dried in the house.

I have to admit that I did enjoy my school years. I started at the National Church of England School when I was four and a half years old. In those days you had to wait for a vacancy to occur before you could make an early start. The Headmistress (Miss Fieldhouse) was a kindly old soul who was ready for retiring and she was soon replaced by Miss Shacklock. The teachers I well recall as being Mrs. Britton, Miss Howell and Mrs. Twydale. In the juniors it was Miss Baker, Mrs. Levin and Mrs. Parkes and, in the Seniors, it was Mr. Raven and Mr. Varley with the Headmaster being Mr. C.S. Harris.

Our family belonged to the Parish Church of Saint Mary Magdalene, where we used to worship regularly and attend special services with the school. It was located in the centre of town in the Market Square. The school motto was painted high over the main arch in the Assembly Halls and read *"MANNERS MAKETH MAN"*. I think in our school years it was probably easier to put into practice than in today's world where it's a case of survival of the fittest and you lose out if you try to follow the motto.

I recall visiting New York in 1943 during my time with the Royal Navy, something which is covered as part of my recollection of my wartime experiences. To illustrate my comments in the previous paragraph, I feel it appropriate to mention my experience when I went into a drugstore to purchase a gift to bring home. I said *"Can I have a so and so please"* and, when I received it, I said *"Thank you very much"* as I'd been brought up to do. To my surprise the fellow behind the counter said, *"Don't thank me, brother, you're paying for it."* A polite *"You are welcome"* would have been much friendlier and appropriate don't you think? I have never forgotten my manners and hope I never do! I am sure that manners do make the man.

Religious instruction, both at school and in church, always played a big part in my life and my faith has always been very strong. Although we were brought up within the Church of England we did attend other denominational services. These included Wesleyan, Reform, Baptist and the Salvation Army – we floated with the best! You name it, my family tried it!

I remember seeing the Salvation Army at their early evening outdoor meetings on the Market Square in Hucknall. I knew many of the old stalwarts and greatly admired them for their faith and commitment. One incident I shall never forget was watching the aging Lady Tudbury sing, with such gusto, "O Boundless Salvation, Deep Ocean of Love". She sang with such feeling that I felt surely that such faith assured her of a place in the Kingdom of Heaven. This hymn has been one of my favourites ever since.

Our love for our mother grew as we grew older. The 1926 General Strike came along and brought new problems for everyone throughout the land but we did, regularly, get a midday meal at the communal soup kitchen. Ours happened to be ideally situated in the band room at the top of Annesley Road, approximately 400 yards from our home. When the school bell rang at noon for lunch, we would dash up the road and Mother would be standing on the doorstep with our cups, plates and cutlery in hand so that we could be early for first sitting.

There was always a friendly, welcoming atmosphere there. It was a "united we stand" spirit, so to speak, and on occasions they would hold social evenings with talent competitions and prizes. It was here that I found I had a good voice and, as a result, I became a "Boy Soprano" winning several prizes, which were always welcome. Patriotic songs always went down well and I brought the house down with my rendition of a firm favourite "Your England and Mine" and a good old rousing school song, "Billy Boy", as an encore. This was,

I'm sure, my first taste of show business which, in later life, led to the love of my social life – the theatre.

Hucknall Co-Operative Society engaged me to "fill the bill" at many of their monthly concerts with a very talented character actor and monologist called Harry Slater. We travelled all around the Nottingham area for many months and, before long, solo spots came along quickly for charity concerts and chapel anniversaries each year. School plays and concerts further fostered my interest but I was never able to attend a pantomime or play on the professional stage because we could not afford it.

I never went to the seaside until I was ten years old and then it was only a day visit to Mablethorpe with the Band of Hope from the church hall. Luckily for us that the sea was in for the few hours we were there!

There were thirteen houses in the small area where we lived, seven on the main road itself and six on the side street. At the rear was a reasonably sized space where everyone used to hang out the washing so it was always put to good use, particularly by my mother. However, I can never recall anyone washing on a Sunday.

After Sunday school in the afternoon, we kids put this "*big yard*", as we used to call it, to good use. It was games time from around four o'clock until dusk and, with at least four kids to every household, we had plenty of competitors for every event. Sometimes, however, we would go for long walks in the countryside taking a bottle of water and a jam sandwich for our tea. We covered miles without any thought of danger and we seemed to use our leisure time to the full. There was never enough time to be bored!

In the evenings we used to design and peg rugs. We were very proud of our creations and often used to get orders for them. I recall my sister Annie and I put a lot of time and thought into one which we thought was our best ever. We worked for weeks to bring it to perfection and carried it the length of Papplewick Lane only to be kept waiting at the door in the freezing cold. We were given three shillings for our trouble and a piece of caraway seed cake which we both hated. What a disappointment!

Annie and I were very close, as we were until her death. We were bosom buddies and went everywhere together doing small jobs and errands for people so that we could put money into Mother's concertina purse. One of our more lucrative enterprises was to go horse mucking where we would follow the horses, even at our age, and charge four pence for a barrow load of manure – there was no such thing as packaged compost or fertiliser back then. Some days business was good, especially if Shipstone's horses were in the area pulling the drays delivering booze to the local pubs. There were also off days when we would barely get half a barrow load.

Not to be beaten, we would dry it off and fluff it up so that it looked like a full load, then we would sprinkle it with water to freshen it up before we took it to our customers. It always worked and so another four pence went into the family coffers. Everyone who had a barrow around at the time of the General Strike found it a blessing in disguise. We would go to the pit banks, searching around for bits of coal to keep the home fires burning, and when this got scarce through being over-picked, we would take a bucket of water with us and wet the coal dust to make small nuggets to put on the fire. Anything to keep us warm and so help our mother.

Annie and I had a love for caring for the elderly. We spent a lot of time with the old and lonely, doing odd jobs and errands for them and also finding time to stay for a chat. It was a rich gift which we are blessed with even to this day. One old dear looked forward to seeing us before we went to school; we would make her a cup of tea and so start her day for her. In the evening we would return to draw her blinds and make her comfortable before going home. Needless to say she was surrounded with sons and daughters who had all done well for themselves but had very little time for their mother. To us she was like the Granny we could never remember having.

Prior to this, however, I had a job in a motor cycle and gramophone shop not far from my home but this only lasted for a few weeks. I received eight shillings per week, working every day from 8am to 6pm and Saturday's from 8am until midday. Sometimes I babysat for the proprietor and his wife to earn a few coppers more. My boss was a keen dirt track motor cycle competitor and went to every meeting – he was the local champion and had won many trophies. I was asked to clean his bikes after each event, a job I did not relish at all. They were kind to me in a way but the wage was so poor for the hours I worked that I decided I just had to leave, so the pit won out after all.

I had barely got established in this new job, but not really liking it, when there was a slump in the industry and our hours were drastically cut back. The pits at the time were privately owned and we were paid by the hours we worked, something the management monitored very carefully. They would get us to be there at 6am but send us home at 9am therefore robbing us of the opportunity to sign on the dole for that day which meant we lost our dole money too. This would happen regularly – so much for private enterprise and no wonder we fought for the Unions and, subsequently, nationalisation took over. The miners in those days really had an axe to grind.

Dad was a little chap, small of stature, but he had a powerful voice. He was a likeable, friendly character, always "Hail fellow, well met", especially to his boozing pals. As a father he was very tolerant and seldom chastised us probably because we never gave him cause to if you can believe that? He would occasionally threaten us with a belting but it never happened as Mother would always take over and smooth things out. I cannot remember him giving me anything, not even encouragement and, as for love, I don't think he or Mother had enough to give away. Life was always an eternal struggle.

Dad's powerful voice got him an annual job announcing the events at the Co-Op Gala and Sports Day, held on the spacious Moor Road ground at Papplewick. We always knew where Dad was when we were there and could regularly hear him putting his aitches in the wrong place. We loved this day and took part in many of the races but, most enjoyable of all, was the bag of goodies we were given. It was quite a package and included cakes, trifle, chocolate and drinks – all free! We were not used to this so it was always a day to remember.

Our treat of the week was on a Friday night, Dad's payday if indeed he managed to bring any home. We were allowed a cake of our choice from Lees, the pastry shop down the road. On my way to school every Friday morning, I used to pause outside their window and think "*What shall I have tonight?*" It was usually a cream horn or éclair but, when the time came, I always changed my mind and settled for a Nelson's Square because it was more filling and lasted longer.

Treats did not come too often when we were kids. Visits to the cinema were rare although we did sometimes manage a Saturday afternoon matinee at the Scala down the road. It was a lovely, intimate little theatre and cost a penny in the chicken run, the area down in the front nearest the screen. A wooden barrier separated this from the plush seats which were tuppence. The chicken run got filled up first and if it was a popular feature, and business was good, they would open a gate in the centre aisle and take some lucky penny customers into the plush. It was, however, the only way of getting to the toilets which were at the back of the auditorium. Inevitably there was always a steady stream of crafty kids who used this as an excuse to go to the toilet and finally end up in the better seats. I did it, so I know!

A passageway from Annesley Road to Ogle Street ran the full length of the cinema and there were three emergency exit doors opening onto the passage. The door nearest the screen end was the most popular spot and, if you pressed your eye against the door joint, you had a good view of the film. Lots of kids knew about it and sometimes you had to wait your turn for a free peep. It was so popular and, because of this, I'm sure there were more "*slant eyed kids*" in our area than anywhere else in the country.

The programmes, at these matinees, were all silent films as talkies had not been invented. They usually consisted of an adventure film and a Three Stooges type comedy with "Haunted Houses" and "The Adventures of Pearl White" being particular favourites of mine. The adventure always rounded off the afternoon with a gripping finale spoiled only by the caption "*To be continued next week*". Inevitably the hero would always rescue his heroine from their latest predicament and he lived to fight another week.

"*School days, school days, good old golden rule days*" we used to sing, but were they? We often used to wonder as it is said they are the happiest days of your life! That is a very debatable point as far as I'm concerned. I didn't dislike it but there were some subjects which were not my forte. Maths, sports and gardening gave me little joy and, to this day, I am not the slightest bit interested. I did however like history, geography, poetry, music, English and religious instruction - the latter won me an award when I was only twelve years old. A lovely Lord Wharton's Bible was presented to me in 1928 for proficiency in the subject and it is still a prized possession within my family today.

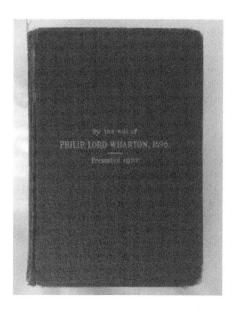

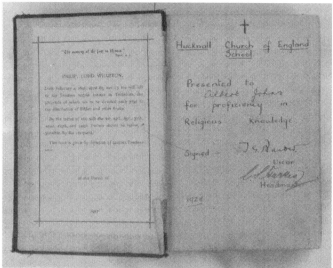

Lord Wharton's Bible, Awarded to Albert in 1928

These bibles were bequeathed by the will of Philip, Lord Wharton, who died on 4 February 1696 at the age of eighty three. He left certain estates in Yorkshire and the proceeds from their sale were to be devoted each year to the distribution of bibles and other books. By the terms of his will, psalms 1, 15, 25, 37, 101, 113 and 145 should be learned, if possible, by the recipient. I read them as often as I could but I thought it would be an impossible task, at the time, with the other school subjects to contend with.

I did have my own favourite bible stories, for instance Kings Chapter 17, which I read time and time again. It seemed to relate to my life as it was unfolding then.

An extract, perhaps illustrating the point, is verses 12 to 16 which reads as follows:

..... *"I don't have any bread, only a handful of flour in a jar and a little olive oil in a jug. I am gathering a few sticks to take home and make a meal for myself and my son, that we may eat it and die".*

Elijah said to her "Don't be afraid. Go home and do as you have said. But first make a small loaf of bread for me from what you have and bring it to me. And then make something for yourself and your son".

For this is what the Lord, the God of Israel says : "The jar of flour will not be used up and the jug of olive oil will not run dry until the day the Lord sends rain on the land".

She went away and did as Elijah had told her. So there was food every day for Elijah and for the woman and her family. For the jar of flour was not used up and the jug of oil did not run dry, in keeping with the word the Lord had spoken to Elijah." ......

The widow, with her handful of corn and a cruse of oil, gave her last to Elijah. She didn't count the cost and, subsequently, she was rewarded by him bringing her son back to life.

In looking through this sixty-year-old treasured possession of mine, Lord Wharton's Bible, I came across a faint, barely indistinguishable message on the back page. I cannot ever recall seeing this before and do not recognise the handwriting. As the Bible has never been out of my possession since it was first presented to me, I do not know from whence it came. It reads:

"*Be not ashamed of the testimony of Christ. He that is ashamed of me, and my name, him will I be ashamed of*". It gives one food for thought don't you think?

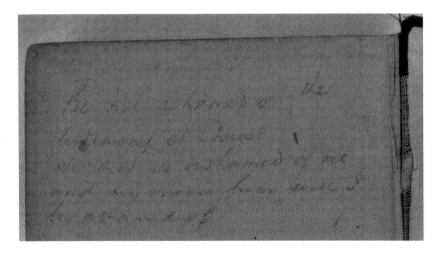

Faint Inscription at the Back of Albert's Bible

ACT TWO – THE WAR YEARS – 1941-1945

BY ALBERT JOHNS, EDITED BY GRAHAM & MURRAY JOHNS

Scene One – The Call-Up and Training

Everyone, like myself, was a new recruit and on New Year's Day 1941 the Battle of Britain was at its height. Norway, Austria, Czechoslovakia, Poland, Hungary, Romania and France were all under the Nazi heel. The unforgettable retreat from Dunkirk was over and so the enemy was literally on our doorstep. Never had England been so near to being conquered during the War as it was then.

I was called to the colour on this day, a fine start to the New Year I thought! I had expected it, but not so soon. I chose the Royal Navy and was pleased when I had to report to *H.M.S. Collingwood*, a shore establishment at Fareham, eight miles outside Portsmouth, on that cold January day. My colleagues had been drawn from all walks of life.

Albert in Uniform

Our disciplinary course, which would normally have taken eighteen months, was completed in ten weeks. During this time Portsmouth was blitzed on 10 January and 10 March with many minor raids in between, so we spent most of our time either in the shelters or cleaning up the debris.

My first leave was a happy experience and I was really proud of the uniform I was wearing. I had to report to *H.M.S. Excellent*, Britain's premier Gunnery School for training, after leave was over. It was an eighteen day strict course and we had to be ready. I passed with 87 marks out of a possible 100 and so, in theory, was considered ready for draft. I was looking forward to life on the big battleships, destroyers and frigates, but fate decreed this was not to be the case.

Hucknall Brothers Choose Service on Land, Sea and In the Air

Here are the portraits of two Hucknall brothers who represent the Royal Navy and Army. On Saturday their youngest brother registered with the 19 years old class and gave his preference for the R.A.F. Soon, therefore, the parents—Mr. and Mrs. Gilbert Johns, of 121, Annesley Road, may have a son in each of the fighting services.

O.S. Albert Johns, the eldest son, who is 24, was called to the

O.S. ALBERT JOHNS

colours on January 1, 1941, and is now making good headway in the Royal Navy. In civilian life he was employed by Messrs. Bairnswear, Ltd., of Perry Road,

Nottingham, where he will be remembered for his interest in the amateur dramatic society there.

Lance-Corporal Harry Johns, the second son, joined the forces on his 21st birthday when the

L/CPL. HARRY JOHNS

war began and he was in France and took part in the unforgettable Dunkirk evacuation. Since then he has been in London for four months, being in the Pioneer Corps.

Both are doing well and are happy; they look forward to the local news in the "Dispatch," which they receive weekly. The youngest son who registered on Saturday, is Mr. Walter Johns.

Local Newspaper Article (Source Unknown)

At the final parade before we disbanded, the Commanding Officer congratulated us on the progress we had made. He then asked for volunteers for D.E.M.S. However, every rookie had been told never to volunteer for anything and there was a deathly silence.

He said "*Right, you, you, you, and you over there are now D.E.M.S.!*" This was repeated until he had assembled fifty unlikely candidates. None of us had heard of this branch of the Royal Navy so we were in for a big surprise. At first I consoled myself by thinking it may be a good number. Every major city in Britain was being bombed at that time, so maybe we would be helping to clear up after these raids. What a stroke of luck - we may never have to leave these shores - but this was not to be. We were still Royal Naval ratings, loaned to the Merchant Navy to defend the cargo ships and troop carriers against enemy action. We were subsequently to learn the following:

D.E.M.S. was an abbreviation for Defensively Equipped Merchant Ships.

What an overstatement this was if ever there was one because we had very little in the way of armaments with which to defend ourselves. When we had been in this unit for a while we realised the Merchant Navy was a front line target and we jokingly called it "*Death Early My Sons*", but this turned out to be too true to be funny.

We were to be transported to ports all over the world and none of us knew where we would finally be operating. To cushion the shock of it all we were given embarkation leave and so I was married at Lenton Abbey Church at 3pm on Monday 9 June 1941 to Miss Ethel Robinson of that Parish. The reception was held at Marsdens' café on Milton Street in Nottingham with a number of friends and family present.

Albert & Ethel on their Wedding Day in 1941

With no time for a honeymoon, the leave was over all too soon. I was recalled to barracks and found I was to catch the train to Gourock (a port on the Clyde) to board, as a passenger, the *S.S. Puɫaski*, a Polish vessel of 12,000 tonnes with accommodation for 750 passengers in peace time.

There were 1,100 troops and their kit aboard when we sailed at 9pm on that Saturday night. My father's prediction that I should sail across the oceans because of my two crowns was about to begin.

It was a moment of excitement as we got underway, tinged with an element of sadness as Scotland disappeared from view. Where we were bound for nobody knew. How long we would be away from home was an even bigger mystery. Many were never to return.

It was a large convoy, mainly troop ships such as the *Empress of Japan* and the *Queen of Bermuda*. Our first glimpse of a foreign country was on 13 July when we arrived at Freetown in Sierra Leone.

We lay off shore for four days whilst we took on fuel and stores. We were not allowed on shore, I suppose for security reasons.

The natives kept us entertained as they circled the ship in their small craft selling their wares and begging us to throw coins in the water so they could dive for them. They never missed, I'm glad to say. Others would sing for us in their own inimitable way; their versions of "Just Molly and Me" and "She'll Be Coming Round the Mountain".

It was up anchor and away on 17 July and we crossed the equator at 9:30am two days later. We did have a small "crossing the line" ceremony, a customary tradition for those who cross for the first time. This takes the form of a severe ducking from King Neptune but, on this occasion, the ship was far too crowded to do this on a large scale.

Because of the overcrowding many people were suffering from dysentery and malaria, so the sick bays were always full and so were the toilets. We were all first time sailors and some suffered very badly from sea sickness. It affected me but not as much as it did some of the others. We all longed to see land again and go ashore. It was then we were told we should be reaching Cape Town and 350 would be taken off to ease the situation. I'm glad to say that I was one of them. I was relieved and overjoyed at the prospect.

However, my joy was to be short-lived when, after two days in lovely Cape Town, the authorities changed their plans and we were told to carry on to Durban where the same number would be taken off. That small journey, however, was gruelling as it was the monsoon season and going round the Cape of Good Hope is no easy task at the best of times. Things got very much worse and as we arrived in Durban a fleet of ambulances were waiting to take patients away.

Army transport was waiting to take off the 350 who were put into Clairwood Transit Camp, just outside the city, to await another ship. Incidentally, we still did not know where we were bound for. I can say however that South Africa is a lovely country. The people of Cape Town and Durban welcomed us with open arms, many begging us to go and settle there when the war was over. We were not confined to the transit camp whilst we were in Durban as we had no duties to perform, so we were free to come and go as we pleased. We did, however, have to report each morning in case some new situation had arisen, always keeping our fingers crossed that it had not so we could stay in this peaceful haven as long as possible.

We managed ten days, mostly spent on the glorious beaches by day and the theatres and cinemas by night. We met and made many new friends, in particular Harold, Ben and Doreen Higgins, who were down in Durban for their two weeks summer vacation from Johannesburg. I was not to know this at the time but Harold had relatives in Selston (near Nottingham) and, after the war, he came to live in Nottingham. When I was demobbed and returned to civvy street some five years later, we met after I rejoined my drama group and Harold actually took part in one of the plays we presented. It's a small world isn't it?

Our hearts were heavy when the time came for us to leave Clairwood Camp. We had heard that we were bound for the Middle East and dreaded the idea of another long voyage in a ship like the *Pułaski*. It was the luck of the draw which gave us this short stay in Durban and we considered we were blessed to be able to stay there for a while.

On 10 August 1941 we were to be ready for embarkation once more, this time on the beautiful Dutch liner *Nieuw Amsterdam* which was 37,000 tonnes, and we set sail immediately. The liner was a story in itself with every luxury available to us. There were three large swimming pools, spacious dining halls, nine elevators, a cinema, a concert hall and games rooms. You name it; this liner really was the last word in luxury.

We had plenty of fun, gala sports days were organised and we were able to join in as we were considered to be passengers and had no set duties. There were 4,500 servicemen on board, Navy, R.A.F. and the Army, most of whom were South Africans.

The journey seemed to be over much too soon and we arrived in Suez on 24 August. As we dropped anchor in the harbour we could clearly see the burnt out shell of the liner *Georgic* which had been bombed only recently. And so the active part of my service life was about to begin.

Scene Two – Active Service – The North Africa Campaign

Within a few hours we were boarding the Egyptian State Railway with "state" being the correct word as they really were in a dreadful state. It was a gruelling journey to the D.E.M.S. depot at Port Said. Our draft was the first to use the barracks located in what they called "The Italian School". The natives were not at all welcoming and certainly not to be trusted. The heat was unbearable and the flies annoying. It was obvious the authorities were awaiting our arrival as, within a few days, many of my colleagues were away on duty on the vessels they had to guard.

My turn came on 19 October when I was sent on another train journey. This time it was to Alexandria where I picked up my ship the *Gibel Kebir* which in Greek means "Little mountain" or "Gibraltar". I could hardly believe my eyes when I saw her, such a small tub of 3,000 tonnes needing a lick of paint and looking as if she could hardly keep afloat. The conditions aboard were appalling with no washing or cleaning facilities. A temporary cabin had been erected amidships for the three gunners which was no more than a crate. The food was Greek-style and always smothered in olive oil.

The Ship's compliment consisted of:

- Captain Cortez, a Spaniard who had escaped from his country during the Spanish Civil War, and was now fighting for our cause.
- The First Mate, Vicente Rodinguez, also a Spaniard, with the same ideals as the Captain.
- The Second Mate, Isaac Rosenberg who was a 23-year-old Polish Jew who had escaped from Warsaw.
- The Chief and First Engineer were both Greek.
- One Royal Marine and the three gunners (myself included), all British.

After the splendour and comfort of the *Nieuw Amsterdam* this really brought us down to earth with a bump. We know that war asks sacrifices of us all and so we settled down to what we knew was to be sheer hell. When we asked where we were bound for we had another shock. "*Tobruk*" was the reply, and our cargo was bombs, mines, petrol, gelignite and some stores. What a target we made and any hit from land, sea or the air would have been curtains for us.

The beleaguered garrison of Tobruk was now in the hands of the Allies and it was being served by only two coastal vessels, the *Gibel Kebir* and a captured Italian schooner named the *Maria Giovanni*. Her Captain was an Australian called Pedlar Palmer and, like Captain Cortez of the *Gibel Kebir*, he was bomb happy. They became friendly rivals, hell-bent on keeping the lifeline open to Tobruk at all costs. In the spirit of this friendly rivalry they competed for the honour of who would run the gauntlet the most times and our Captain had done 24 missions when we joined him for the 25th.

On the funnel of this grubby little craft were painted three rats, denoting that his crew were "honourable members" of the garrison. Anyone serving in Tobruk for over three months was allowed to paint a rat on his steel helmet. This came about because of comments made by Lord Haw-Haw in his broadcasts, who used to say "*Where are the Tobruk rats now? Scurrying into their shelters?*"

On Monday afternoon, 20 October, along with one solitary escort vessel, a trawler called the *H.M.S. Wolborough*, we left our base in Alexandria. The tension was bad, alerts and false alarms were many, but at 2:15pm on the Thursday afternoon we heard the drone of enemy planes as they started to dive on us out of the blazing sun. In this way we had little chance of seeing them before they were on us. Nine Stuka bombers came screeching down spraying gunfire along the decks from stem to stern. We were at action stations, but our equipment was pretty useless against their combined fire. All we had was a Bren gun each, set on a single stand with no armour plating to shield us. Thank heavens for our friends on *H.M.S. Wolborough* who put up the main defence.

During this skirmish, one of our colleagues who was manning his gun forward on the fo'c'sle, received a bullet through his right thigh, after firing only three rounds from his own gun. He was a Glaswegian (Jock, we always called him) and he was very courageous as we made him comfortable amidships. Jerry returned again at 5:15pm still intent on putting us below. This time he dropped bombs which fell so near the ship they made our teeth chatter in their sockets. A direct hit could have been disastrous for us all, considering the cargo we were carrying.

The following is a clipping from the Egyptian Mail about the incident after the Captain had been interviewed by a reporter on his return to Alexandria:

London, November 8.

The Spanish Republican airman, Captain Cortez, who flew with the squadron that bombed the German pocket-battleship Deutschland in October 1936, has just completed his twenty-fifth voyage to Tobruk as master of a cargo steamer. He has encountered with the Germans several times both in daylight and at night.

The British C.-in-C., Mediterranean, in a message to Captain Cortez says:

"I congratulate you on your very successful voyage to Tobruk. Good work is what I expected from your previous fine performance."

The captain's exploits are in the tradition of the conquistadores who once made the name of Spain great. His ship is neither of the newest, nor of the fastest design. His first officer is a political refugee from Spain. His second is a Polish Jew, and men and officers alike man guns and automatic weapons.

Attacked three times during daylight, shelled as she entered harbour and bombed and shelled throughout the night and the next day, his ship discharged her cargo. Then she left harbour and undertook another 24 hour's battling before she got clear of the danger zone and set course home through friendlier waters.

Captain Cortez said:

"It is nothing to us. We have nothing more to lose except our lives."

"German No Like It"

Talking of how they clipped pieces off the wing of one of the three Messerschmitts 109 which dived on them, he said:

"We no can see them, but I get my big gun straight in the sun because I know they are there. I am all the time working the machine-gun to throw a cone of bullets where they must be. I hear the noise of them diving, but still no see. Then a third machine come straight. I say fire. German no like it. He climbed off so hard, his engines scream louder than the sound of gun. Pieces from his starboard wing drop off and one fall on our deck. Beautiful." — (B.O.P.).

At this point I think it is worth a minor detour in my narrative to possibly explain the inbuilt hatred the Captain and First Mate had towards the Germans. At the time I was unaware of events during the Spanish Civil War and I'm sure many of you will fall into this category. I subsequently made it my business to find out more with a view to possibly explaining their hostility.

Suffice to say it was a very brutal and divisive affair. Families were split apart and provinces were either pro- or anti-Franco. Adolf Hitler was a big supporter of Franco's cause whilst Franco himself allowed the Führer to undertake major atrocities within Spain which alienated many of the anti-Franco brigade.

One of the worst of these occurred on 26 April 1937 in the small town of Guernica, situated approximately 30km east of Bilbao in the Basque area of Northern Spain. It was market day and there were reputed to be more than 10,000 people gathered in the town. Reports of fatalities vary from between c. 130 to 1,600.

In essence the Luftwaffe, at the request of the Spanish Nationalists, was allowed to trial the practice of "Terror Bombing", a policy in which civilians were deliberately targeted in order to break the will of the people and aid the possible collapse of an army (evidently, at the time of the attack, Basque Republican forces were at the front line to the east of Guernica).

Events in Guernica were to be the inspiration for Picasso's mural sized oil painting which was completed in June 1937. It depicts the suffering of both humans and animals and the painting, part of a touring exhibition, was used to raise funds for Spanish War Relief, became widely acclaimed and helped raise worldwide attention of the Spanish Civil War.

On the evidence of what I saw I think it's fair to say that both the Captain and First Mate fell into the classification of Republican as they hated Hitler, and of course Franco, and everything they stood for. This, no doubt, accounted for their presence on the *Gibel Kebir*.

We finally reached Tobruk at 1:30am on Friday morning. We entered the harbour under cover of darkness. Jock was hurriedly taken to hospital ashore and sadly that was the last we ever heard of him. As dawn broke we went on deck to review the situation. Tobruk harbour was a graveyard of bombed and burnt out hulks of derelict ships. We were told there were 64 in all at that time – British, German, Italian and Greek.

As the war progressed the occupation of Tobruk had changed hands several times. I recall some of the names of these wrecks - the *Serenitas*, *Liguria*, and the battle cruiser *San Giorgio* were Italian and the *Draco* and *Chantala* were British. We were alongside the *Serenitas* to discharge our cargo and camouflaged to look like a wreck, but I don't really think this was necessary as we were a wreck in every sense of the word.

The Germans had a powerful gun they called "Bardia Bill" situated out on the headland at Bardia which they still occupied. It was capable of lobbing huge shells at a terrific rate, so it controlled our activities in the harbour. Any small movement meant they would open up a barrage causing much damage and many casualties, besides being a nuisance. We had to report to Navy House and, in doing so, saw evidence of this damage. Few buildings, if any, were standing and everybody lived in underground shelters. As night fell on the second day we were advised to join the army in the shelters, heavy night raids being forecast. We were pleased about this so we could at least get some sleep.

By the end of the third day we were unloaded and ready for off. We were to be towed – by *H.M.S. Wolborough* – as our compass and other instruments had been damaged on one of these raids. It was vital we get out of German occupied territory waters before daylight.

We managed without any major incident and arrived back in Alexandria two days later.

My first, and the *Gibel Kebir's* 25th, successful voyage to Tobruk was completed. I heaved a huge sigh of relief and thanked God for a safe return, not knowing that I had to do the November and December journeys too. We were allowed shore leave whilst the ship was being repaired, restocked and reloaded so we were able to explore the nicer parts of Alexandria and, in doing so, met many of the English-speaking community. They always made us welcome, which is more than we could say about the Egyptians.

I was surprised just how disliked and unpopular we Brits were wherever we went. I was told by those who had been in Egypt for some time that they ebbed and flowed with the tide of war. If the Germans were winning and near their borders, they had Nazi flags ready to welcome them. As long as we were there to defend them from that happening they tolerated us, but only just.

19 November 1941 and we were ready once again to run the blockade to Tobruk. "The Big Push", as it was termed, had just started and the Allies had routed Jerry out of Sallum. As we hugged the coastline we could see the exchange of gunfire and hear the aircraft going over from Italy on their raids. The voyage was not without incidents and tense moments.

I was glad we arrived safely as our cargo was the Christmas fare for the boys who were making such a gallant effort in this siege. The Allies had taken many prisoners in the push of the 19th and we brought back the first batch of prisoners on our return - 180 Germans and 46 Italians.

We listened to their stories from those who could speak a little English. They were so confident that victory would be theirs and very soon too. They assured us that Moscow had fallen but we assured them that it had not. When they saw our naval strength in Alexandria their spirits were not so high, but their war was at an end. They were sent to a P.O.W. camp in the Red Sea area. No one knew it at that time but the war had four more years to run.

A dangerous cargo of high explosives was our load for the December run which started on the 17th. We hoped for a quiet and peaceful run with no incidents if at all possible. We were accompanied by the *S.S. Zealand*, which was making her first run. We had to be on the alert all the way, but we made it in good time to spend Christmas Eve with the lads in the shelters. By now they were beginning to know us all and always looked forward to our arrival. Fire broke out on the *S.S. Zealand* whilst unloading but it was brought under control.

Our Christmas with the lads was very short lived as, on 27 December, we were on the return journey carrying 515 prisoners, mostly Italians.

There was a small convoy of small ships like ours, with the *S.S. Volo* in charge and a few tank landing craft. It was bitterly cold and sandstorms were raging but blowing out to sea, which afforded us a certain amount of cover. We were pleased about this as the moon was high. At 3am we heard a terrific explosion and saw that the *S.S. Volo* had been hit. The convoy hurriedly dispersed and we could see the battle going on between a destroyer and a submarine. Flares were sent up and depth charges dropped which brought the sub to the surface. We later learned fourteen of our men survived off the *Volo* and many prisoners were taken off the submarine. The rest of the journey continued without incident, arriving back on New Year's Day 1942. It was a happy day for me as I learned I was to be taken off the *Gibel Kebir*.

What a year it had been, so much had been packed into so short a time. I welcomed in 1942 but it was wishful thinking. I'm afraid I was to be very disappointed!

Albert Johns

Scene Three – Indian Ocean and Back

How I wished at times that I had been in the Royal Navy, especially when I went into barracks waiting for my next draft. D.E.M.S. was a lonely life really as we had very little in common with the merchant seamen. Whilst in barracks I would go along with other mates to their shore-based activities and often visited them aboard their battleships which were in port. During this period I met seven servicemen from my home town of Hucknall – Harold Hayes, Howard Runacus, Jim Ball, John Holmes, Sam Bakewell, Wilf Lawson and Tom Berridge – and we spent several happy nights together. Jim was to be married and I had an invitation to the wedding but, sadly, duty made it impossible for me to attend.

At this time I received an urgent message from my brother-in-law and I went to visit him multiple times. The following is a report from the local newspaper:

90-Mile Desert Hike To See Sick Brother-In-Law

A COALVILLE airman, lying in hospital in the desert, had a visit from his sailor brother-in-law, who had hitch-hiked 90 miles across the desert to be at his bedside.

A.C.1 Arthur Cross, whose home is in Crescent-road, Hugglescote, had been serving in the Middle East for some time, when he received a letter from his brother-in-law, Able Seaman Albert Johns, of Hucknall, Notts., stating that he was in the Middle East.

They arranged to meet, but two days before the appointed day, Aircraftman Cross was admitted to hospital with serious injuries.

A member of the hospital staff arranged for a letter to be sent to Seaman Johns, cancelling the appointment.

Arthur Cross and Albert Johns

Soon after receiving the letter, the sailor obtained 48 hours' leave and unable to reach the hospital by any other means, he hitch-hiked 90 miles across the desert to see his pal.

Aircraftman Cross remained in hospital for five months, during which time Seaman Johns did the 90-miles journey on five more occasions, walking part of the way and begging lifts from any vehicle.

During one of these visits, on Whit-Sunday, Aircraftman Cross was given leave from hospital. The two boys spent a happy time and celebrated by being photographed together, as pictured here.

Aircraftman Cross is coming home shortly. He formerly worked in a Leicester boot factory.

On 19 January it was off again to Tobruk. This time on the Greek vessel the *S.S. Manoula* which was 5,000 tonnes. Our only escort on this occasion was *H.M.S. Peony*, a mine sweeper. The weather was foul and visibility very poor. We ran aground off Sallum and the *Peony* did a sweep round us and then did the same thing in shallower water. Tugs were sent to our aid from Mersa Matruh, but it was three days before we were both re-floated and able to complete our journey.

Rommel and the Germans were now at Benghazi and ready for another assault on Tobruk so after a quick turnabout we discharged our cargo and made our way back. When we arrived in Alexandria, I was taken off the *Manoula* and away from the Middle East Campaign in the Mediterranean.

On 26 February I was commissioned onto the Norwegian ship *S.S. Goviken* (5,000 tonnes) and our destination was Lourenço Marques in Portuguese East Africa. The ship's company was:

- Captain: Georg Heldal of Bergen.
- First Officer: Ole Gjertsen of Oslo.
- 2nd Officer: Nils Rasmussen of Hauge.
- 3rd Officer: Georg Gulbrandsen of Tromso.
- Chief Engineer: Isak Olsen of Oslo.
- Crew of 43 Chinese from Hong Kong and Swatow in China.

This ship had operated on the China coast for four years and had not encountered any war action at all. She was fitted out with armaments and we three gunners were the first defence personnel ever assigned to the ship. We did the one successful journey down to Lourenço Marques, and returned without incident. Everyone aboard seemed to get very complacent.

After a quick turn round we were off again, presumably on the same mission, but we made several diversions. We called at Massawa in Eritrea, the last stand by the Italians in the Abyssinian Campaign. There was lots of evidence of this as we entered the harbour, where there were 37 wrecks and a huge dry dock out of action. It was unbearably hot and we were pleased when we were put to sea again. Our next port of call was to be Aden (then a British Crown colony) and we had a new enemy to contend with in the Red Sea as we were attacked by a plague of locusts. It was a horrible experience while it lasted and the only thing to do was run for cover until it was over.

As we entered the Indian Ocean the monsoon season was beginning. We had taken ballast on at Aden because of this, 700 tonnes of salt to keep us stable in the water. The journey was slow and monotonous, we could do no more than four knots because of the gale force winds and the rain. We three gunners had exhausted every topic of conversation we could think of as we had been together for so long. The Norwegians were limited in their knowledge of English and their sense of humour was totally different to ours. The Chinese were a law unto themselves and at times disregarded blackout regulations, having never seen any action since their arrival in this area; and we had no escort with us to remind them of this.

We had heard that the Japanese submarines were operating off Mauritius and in the Mozambique Channel, the area which we were about to enter. The Captain had warned us of this, but the crew were still very careless. We three gunners were naturally concerned, as it was our duty to defend the *Goviken*. We did have the Royal Navy to escort us in the Mediterranean, but it was not considered necessary in the Indian Ocean. We were restless for days and seemed to sense something was about to happen. We made ourselves comfortable below the aft mounted gun so we would be ready in the event of anything happening.

The situation was not improved much when Gunner Albert Frankel, from Birmingham, came to breakfast on the Saturday morning and said, "*I don't like to tell you blokes this but I dreamt we'd been tin-fished* (that was naval slang for being torpedoed). *We all got in the lifeboat together but Frank* (Blagborough, the other gunner who came from Manchester) *dived over the side after his hat!*" We laughed uneasily about this, but thought about the old wives saying "*Friday night's dream, Saturday told, sure to come true before nine days old*". Within three days this is exactly what did happen!

At 9.40pm on Monday, 29 June, the *S.S. Goviken* was torpedoed off Madagascar. The torpedo struck right underneath our accommodation aft, blowing the propeller and rudder off. Frank, the gunner, was on watch at the time whilst Albert Frankel and I were in a recess under the gun. The weather was foul and the rain was torrential. We never seemed to relax after being told about the dream and you can tell how we felt because despite the bad weather we decided to sleep on deck and as near to the gun as we possibly could; and it's a good job we did as our cabin was below the gun where we slept and it was there that the torpedo struck. I recall being blown off my feet, the lifeboat near us being blasted away, fragments of which hit my nose and hips and I seemed to lose all sense of bearing until I heard a voice shout "*Johnny, follow me!*" They called me Johnny, my surname being Johns.

We ran amidships to lower the lifeboats, a job the crew should have been doing but they were busy saving their belongings. By the time we had lowered it to sea level, twenty five of them had already got in. The Second Officer, and we three gunners, slid down the ropes and managed to get on board. We shoved away and drifted aft. It was then we saw what damage had been done!

We met another lifeboat from the port side with only the third officer and a few crew in it. As we came closer together they called for one of the gunners to go into their boat. Frank was the nearest, so he obliged. This we presume was the part of the dream where he was supposed to have dived over the side after his hat.

After this we heard a swish through the water underneath us, then a blinding flash and an explosion which tossed us around like corks. It seemed very strange to me that the second torpedo should explode before reaching the ship. We figured afterwards that it may have hit some debris below water level. We were now enveloped in a cloud of acrid smoke. It was obvious we must get away from the *Goviken* as quickly as possible. We watched her go slowly down, stern first. When she got into a vertical position, she quickly submerged and was no more. The swell drove all the lifeboats apart and when dawn broke the following day, we were alone.

We did not see, or hear, of any of the other survivors until we met in Cape Town a few weeks later. The second officer, who was in our boat, was on duty when the torpedo struck so he knew the exact position. The compass in the lifeboat was of no use, neither were the pistols, so we were at the mercy of the sea and the elements. We knew if we were to make land we had to go dead west but wind, rain and heavy swells carried us northwards. This went on for two days. We saw lone ships in the offing but they could not see us in such tumultuous seas.

I never for a single moment despaired or thought, "*This is it*". I still had good faith and it was as strong as ever despite what had happened. I learned at school that more things are wrought by prayer than this world dreams of, so I prayed. We had not seen the sun for over a week, but at 11am on the second day the weather improved and so did our hopes that we might make it. At 4:30pm, an hour before sun was about to set, we had drifted into the shipping lanes and were sighted by the Blue Funnel Line *S.S. Phemius*.

Our prayers had been answered and, as we were being helped aboard, I realised this was the first British ship that I had set foot on after eighteen months in the Navy. We were told we had drifted one hundred and twenty miles in two days and would have made the coast of East Africa the following day had we not been picked up. When I say "we", I mean the gunners, one Norwegian second officer, twenty five Chinese seamen and one lovely little puppy dog which the Norwegians had called Bouncer.

Everyone on board was kind and helpful to us and it was good for us to be able to converse with them in our own language. It was also great to have a decent meal, a shower and clean clothing. More than all this we needed a good night's rest. We reported to the sick bay and were examined before turning in for the night, but found it difficult to relax.

The Captain requested a report of the sinking, it was left to me to write with the others signing it:

Seaman Gunners Report on Sinking of SS. COVIKEN

It was on the night of June 29 1942, at approx 22 Hours that a torpedo from an enemy submarine struck the ship, starboard side aft.

The Gunlayer. J. Blagborough was on watch at the time on the gun deck aft, and we the undersigned were sleeping beneath the gun deck. We were awakened by the explosion, to find the No 3 Lifeboat on the starboard side aft was completely smashed, and the ship was slowly submerging astern, and we then saw Blagborough (Ch) who told us he saw no sign of the submarine, and the gun deck was defective owing to the explosion.

We then heard the ships siren and hurriedly went amidships to find the Chinese crew in a panic, but making no effort to get the lifeboats down. We then began to lower the starboard lifeboat amidships and the crew began to clamour in, and when we finally managed to get in ourselves along with the second officer, who was sent by the Captain to join us we found we had a boat load, and more than half the crew.

We pulled away towards aft and saw the other boat, and we recognised the 3rd Officer, and to others in it. He came along side us and Gunlayer Blagborough and two others went over into that boat, and the last we saw of them they were pulling towards the ship to take off those still aboard.

We were drifting away from the ship, when we heard another loud explosion, and saw something burst about 50 yards astern of our boat, sending a shower of sparks up, and afterwards for a few minutes we were not able to see anything owing to being enveloped in a cloud of smoke.

After this we saw the ship again, then — down in the water amidships, and in vertical position, and then no more. We drifted along for 42 Hours, trying to make our way to land and we were finally picked up by S.S. Phemius.

Albert E Frankel AB
C/JX 236508

A.B. Albert Edward Johns
P.J.X. 236976,

We were awakened at 7am by the action station alarm bells! A submarine had been sighted as she fired two torpedoes at the *Phemius*. Timely action by the Captain saved us from being hit. He swerved the ship and the torpedoes went each side. We carried on at a speedy 16 knots. Remember, like every other vessel, we were without a Navy escort. It was not considered necessary, so the enemy just had to lie in wait and peg us off if they could.

We arrived in Cape Town on 10 July and the Naval authorities soon kitted us out and we collected our back pay. We met our colleagues off the *Goviken* who had arrived there a couple of days before. We exchanged stories as we had seen nothing of them since we drifted apart after the sinking. We knew that survivors leave must be on the cards and we were sent to Worcester, a small town a hundred miles from Cape Town. Situated in the Hex River Valley, it was a delightful spot, set amongst farms and lakes with the Hex mountain range in the background.

We were met by a Mrs. Luff and several ladies of their welcoming committee. A Mrs. Crosson was to be Frank and Albert Frankel's hostess and I was to stay with a Mr. and Mrs. Brown. We met many seamen from *H.M.S. Hecla* who were also on leave and were to be guests of these good people. We spent fourteen days of heaven and it was good to get away from it all. We were able to put the horrors of war at the back of our minds for a while. They had planned tours to farms and factories, concerts, dances, morning coffee and afternoon teas and church services. It was over too soon. All good things must come to an end so we had to return to Cape Town and to duty.

We were promised our next draft would take us to England. On Friday, 13 August, I picked up the *S.S. Hindustan*, which was 5,000 tonnes, laden with a cargo of cotton from Egypt to the U.K. They had kept their promise and soon we were underway. Our journey started pleasantly but the donkeyman severed his thumb very badly and needed hospital treatment. We had to pull into Walvis Bay, S.W. Africa for a couple of days. This meant we missed the convoy but met up with them later in Freetown where we were to assemble ready for our final stage of the journey home.

It was 23 September when we arrived in Liverpool. The weather was cold and wet, but that didn't matter. We were home for thirty days with our loved ones but, with so little time and so much to do, and having had no time together since we were married, Ethel and I planned to go places to make up for the lost fifteen months.

This we did, but very soon it was over and so on Monday, 2 November, I had to return to Liverpool to do a two day gunnery course on the new rocket launcher, "The Pill Box", which was hastily being installed on the larger merchant ships and liners. One such ship was the 19,000 tonnes Cunard White Star Liner, the *Scythia* and this was to be my next commission. I joined her, as did 5,000 troops of the 1st Army, bound for who knows where.

There were lots of wild guesses, but no one came up with the right answer. When we got underway we heard of the successful landings in North Africa on 8 November, so it looked as if we were the back-up team for that invasion. In our convoy were twenty eight troopships including *The Duchess of York*, *Letitia*, *Orion*, *Windsor Castle*, *Orontes* and *Staffordshire* to name but a few.

We arrived off Algiers at dawn on Sunday, 22 November. It was a lovely daybreak and as the day progressed it got sunnier. There were a lot of comings and goings, but we had to wait our turn before our troops could disembark. They were told to be at the ready, but nothing materialised that day so it meant another night aboard for them. Night fell and the moon was full – ideal conditions for the enemy who were soon sending over waves of bombers to keep us busy. We began firing at them from 7pm. With such a concentration of troopships and escorts the flack was heavy so we could put up a reasonably effective barrage.

We were anchored about three miles off shore and the destroyers were laying smoke screens around us. There were several lulls in the attacks but they were short lived and one could never relax the watch. At 5:40am, as dawn was breaking, we were struck by an aerial torpedo, right forward in the bows of the ship. The alarm bells sounded as the ship shuddered from the impact. She lurched and seemed to tilt forward. All troops were called on deck in case it became necessary to abandon ship. After hasty inspection it was found this might not be necessary. The damage was in the storage compartments, where all the ships stores and mail was kept. This helped cushion the impact and also wedge the hole made by the torpedo. We were told three ship's personnel were injured and six suffered badly from shock.

The watertight doors were quickly closed to keep the damage to a minimum. Soon we were towed into harbour alongside a vacant jetty and the troops were taken off as quickly as possible. It was obvious the *Scythia* was going to be out of action for quite some time so we prepared ourselves for a long stay in Algiers. It was to occupy this berth for many weeks until she could be taken into dry dock at Gibraltar.

Nightly raids were regular over Algiers and the Naval Barracks ashore was hit on one of these raids. The question was, where would we accommodate those who had survived? The answer was to use the *Scythia* as a temporary hostel.

I got another touch of what it was like in the Navy. In our off-duty hours we had many opportunities for get-togethers on board. Shore leave had been stopped because of the tense situation. Christmas came along and we made the best of everything to try to make it a happy one but, on 24 December, Admiral Darlan was assassinated in Algiers. This did not help matters, but life goes on, so we made the most of Christmas 1942. At one of the get-togethers we organised, I met my cousin who was serving as an R.D.F. rating in the Navy and also an old school mate of mine, Bob Wilmott.

Thankfully the start of the New Year brought some good news as we heard of the rapid progress the 1st and 8th Armies were making in the Western Desert.

Divers had been working on the ship's damage and managed to make her seaworthy to attempt the journey to the dry dock in

Gibraltar. This was not to be easy and the foul weather did not help in any way. Heavy seas gave the temporary repairs a battering so we had to pull into Oran. The Americans were in charge of this port. It had one of the biggest dry docks in the world and their engineers worked feverishly hard to get the ship re-floated. They were in charge of the defence of Oran and as far as we could see they had everything under control. What the fate was of the *Scythia* after this we dared not think, but surprisingly, all the D.E.M.S. ratings were taken off and put in the pool ashore to wait for our next assignment.

They were a good set of blokes. We were an excellent team so we were sorry when the time came for us to disband. It was obvious that from here we would be on those grubby little coasters again, the same as the *Gibel Kebir*, but this time we would be operating from the western end of the Mediterranean.

I did not relish these thoughts, but the way things were going I was correct in my assumptions. Norman Howard, my chum from Manchester, was soon put on the *S.S. Esneh*, running petrol and ammunition to Bône, Bougie and Phillipeville (now Annaba, Béjaïa and Skikda in Algeria respectively). Taffy, a likeable lad, replaced a rating who was sick on the *S.S. Merope*, doing the same run and my best chums of all Frank Bawden and Jimmy Lavender followed suit on the *S. S. Fintra*.

Was this an act of faith, that I should be the one left alone, or had good fortune smiled on me once again? I kept my fingers crossed, hoping the latter would be the answer to that. I had, however, been asked about my service by the C.O. in charge of the pool. When I told him of my exploits in the blockade at Tobruk, he hinted that that alone was enough for any one person and no doubt I would be glad to get out of the Mediterranean.

I never thought our discussion would be the deciding factor of my next assignment and I was kept in the pool for some time. Knowing the missions my friends and colleagues had embarked upon took about three weeks round trip, I was hoping that I might see them before I got drafted, but this was not to be. However, I was over the moon when I was told to join the *S.S. Manchester Commerce*, a 5,000 tonnes vessel which was bound for England. We departed for home on 23 February 1943.

During our short friendship on *Scythia* we had made arrangements that whoever got home first, and this looked as if it was going to be me, would write to the parents of the others and let them know how they were progressing. I was proud to be the one able to do this and wrote off my letters on the journey home, posting them in Salford, where the ship docked after coming up the Manchester Ship Canal. I made my letters as cheerful and newsy as possible, hoping their sons would soon be home to tell their side of it all.

Mrs. Bawden, Frank's mother, wrote back to me by return of post, thanking me for my kindness and thoughtfulness but, at the same time that my letter arrived, she also received the dreaded telegram, which all mothers, wives and sweethearts feared:

"*The Admiralty regret to inform you that your son has been killed by enemy action in the Mediterranean theatre of the war on 23 February 1943.*"

This was the day I had picked up the *Manchester Commerce* for my journey home. Little did I know at the time that my chum was no more. His kindness, thoughtfulness and his coolness whilst in action was an inspiration to all who knew him. Long will I remember him and all my other good friends who made the ultimate sacrifice.

A person's life should not be measured by the material wealth he has gained, but by the wonderful friendships, experiences and memories he has gathered along the way. I did not know it at the time, but on my next voyage, I would begin a friendship which was to last for a long, long time and, as I write this, it is 54 years old (1997).

Scene Four – The North Atlantic

I was glad when I was ordered to return to the *Manchester Commerce* after a short spell of leave. I had heard on the grapevine that she might be returning to her usual peace time run and, if she was to do this, it would suit me fine. The prospects of going over to Canada, and hopefully later, the United States, appealed to me very much. On 1 April 1943 we joined a massive convoy being assembled in the Mersey, all ready for crossing the Atlantic. The destination was to be Saint John, New Brunswick, Canada.

We did not expect a quiet, uneventful, crossing so we were not surprised when the enemy was there in full force. On 11 April, after much action, *H.M.S. Beverley* was sunk, and the following night, the *S.S. Lancastrian Prince* met her doom in the same way. It was a relief when we arrived at our first port of call, Halifax, Nova Scotia, on Canada's Eastern Seaboard. It didn't look much of a place from the ship, it looked like a large fishing community, but it had a natural, strategic position for convoy assembly and dispersal. I was told that, in the First World War, a cargo ship loaded with ammunition blew up in the harbour causing considerable damage and loss of life. The wooden buildings ashore had been knocked down as if they were skittles. There was no time to go ashore because we only stayed overnight as we were due in Saint John on Good Friday and to spend Easter there.

New Brunswick is one of the Maritime Provinces, better known to Canadians as the "Picture Province". The capital is Fredricton, but Saint John prides itself as being Canada's first city. It is as British as the Union Jack and its inhabitants were more loyal to the Crown than many of us in Britain today. These wonderful, kind and friendly people welcomed us with open arms and open doors to their homes.

I was adopted, if that is the right word, by Mr. and Mrs. Lutton and their daughter Lois. Their home was mine, along with my colleagues and other Allied servicemen, whilst we were in port. The Lutton family looked upon this as their contribution to the war effort and we, who had been away from home for so long, really appreciated what they were doing for us. We enjoyed a taste of home life whilst we were in this port and were very grateful to our hosts and their friends. This was the beginning of the friendship I mentioned earlier.

The turn round of the ship to unload and reload usually took approximately ten days. Because of the Easter recess we gained an extra two days leave. We had no duties to do, only to report to the ship each day to see what progress was being made. We need not have done this as Mr. Lutton worked for the Canadian Pacific Railway and Saint John was the largest marshalling yard on the east coast for vital goods being transported to the U.K. and European war zones.

He kept us informed as to the progress the *Commerce* was making and told us what cargo we would be taking. This time it was general cargo for the U.K. He told us to relax and enjoy ourselves for a few more days.

Mrs. Lutton was a charming person and an excellent cook. Her dear old mother, Granny Griffiths, lived with them. She came from a long line of seafaring people and her husband had been a Captain. Lois, their only daughter, and her friends organised many outdoor events during the day and parties and dances in the evenings. We crammed a lot into that twelve days, not wanting it to end. With such a welcome we were sad when the time came for us to leave, but I always say, if there were no endings there would never be any beginnings, would there?

And so, on 2 May 1943, it was cast off to make our way back to Halifax to join the convoy home. As we steamed past the coast of Newfoundland the air was very cold.

We knew there were icebergs in the area and we saw a number of medium and small-sized ice floes. The most beautiful sight of all was the Aurora Borealis (the Northern Lights) which lit up the skies. It was to be an "on the alert" journey back home. There were signals coming through of packs of U-Boats waiting to strike but nothing serious happened, I'm pleased to say.

I made this same trip to Saint John in July, arriving back in August. I could not wait to get in touch with the Luttons and rang them as soon as the ship docked. A strange voice answered and told me there was no one at home. They were paying their last respects to Granny Griffiths who had passed away earlier that week. I apologised for interrupting them in their grief and the lady said she would give them my message. I said I would call them the next time I was in port.

However, before the day was out, I got a message from Mr. Lutton saying "*Please come up, all of you, and behave exactly as you did before. I know your company will do Elizabeth* (Mrs. Lutton) *a world of good at this time*". This we did and, when we left, he could not thank us enough.

When we arrived back in the U.K. the Prime Minister announced that four million tonnes of merchant shipping had been safely convoyed across the Atlantic without a single loss whilst 90 U-Boats had been destroyed in that period.

In my opening statements relating to being in D.E.M.S. I said I had heard the Merchant Navy was a front line force and seen for myself that this was so, but I never realised just how much life at sea in the Royal Navy and Merchant Navy demanded of you.

It was brought to my notice, with some alarm I may add, when I recently read Alistair MacLean's novel "San Andreas", in which some of his revelations amazed me. He really spells it out in his book, and I quote:

At the outbreak of war in September 1939 the British Merchant Navy was in a parlous state indeed – pitiable would probably be a more accurate term. Most of the ships were old, a considerable number unseaworthy and some no more than rusting hulks, plagued by interminable mechanical breakdowns.

Even so, those vessels were in comparatively good shape compared to the appalling living conditions of those whose misfortune it was to serve aboard those ships. The reason for the savage neglect of both ships and men could be summed up in one word – greed.

The fleet owners of yesteryear – and there are more than a few around today – were grasping, avaricious and wholly dedicated to their high priestess – profit at all costs, provided that the cost did not fall on them.

***

British shipping losses were appalling beyond belief and beggar even the most active imagination. In the first eleven months of war, Britain lost 1,500,000 tonnes of shipping. In some of the early months of 1941, losses averaged close on 500,000 tonnes. In 1942, the darkest period of the war at sea, 6,250,000 tonnes of shipping went to the bottom. Even working at full stretch British shipyards could replace only a small fraction of those enormous losses.

That, together with the fact that the number of operational U-Boats in that same grim year rose from 91 to 212 made it certain that, by the law of diminishing returns, the British Merchant Navy would eventually cease to exist unless a miracle occurred.

The name of that miracle was Liberty Ships

***

As a lifeline, a conduit and an artery, the Liberty Ships were on a par with the British Merchant Navy. Without them Great Britain would *have assuredly gone down in defeat. All the food, oil, arms and ammunition which overseas countries – especially the United States – were eager and willing to supply were useless without the ships in which to transport them.*

I must say that, as a D.E.M.S. rating loaned to merchant shipping, I agree with every word that MacLean has written. Liberty Ships all had the name Sam in their title. The idea being that they were a gift from Uncle Sam. I served on two of these in my later years, the *Samspelga* and the *Samois*.

Albert Johns

Scene Five – Back to North Africa and the Mediterranean

And so my life in this seemingly endless war moved on, but not in the direction that I had hoped it would. It was rumoured that our next run on the *Commerce* would be to Alexandria in Egypt, of all places, and I had left it too late to try to get a move.

As we left England on 28 August we did have some cheerful news to launch us on our way when it was announced that Italy had surrendered to the Allies. At least life in the Mediterranean would be a little easier. It was an unusual convoy and we seemed to get nowhere fast. We hugged the North African coast and could see all the places we had visited earlier on. It was like a conducted tour of all the battlefronts and I, for one, was not interested. Things did liven up, however, when we arrived off Bizerte, when the captured Italian fleet sailed through our convoy. We saw fifty of our bombers going over to bomb Foggia, where the main action was taking place at that time.

As we approached Alexandria, our orders were changed, and we had to continue our journey down the Suez Canal to Port Tewfik, arriving there on 22 September.

Having done this journey so many times in the past there was very little that interested me so I was glad when the ship discharged her cargo and we reloaded again with cotton for the U.K.

We left Suez on 14 October. This time we were to be the Commodore ship and have Royal Navy personnel on board to be in charge of the convoy. All went well until we were off Algiers on 21 October. It was action stations all day long. Depth charges were being dropped for over two hours and, as night fell, we got the message that a large formation of enemy, torpedo-carrying planes, were heading our way.

A smoke screen was laid by the naval vessels which sped up and down the lanes of the convoy. Daylight was quickly fading so this also concealed us from the enemy, and them from us, but all hell seemed to be let loose as the barrage commenced. It lasted for over an hour. Two of our ships were sunk and one crippled – but able to make the safety of Oran. Two aircraft were accounted for and one was a further possibility. Being the Commodore ship, we got this information first-hand.

The following day we passed the Rock of Gibraltar and went out into the Atlantic to join up with another convoy from West Africa which was on its way home. We knew we were being shadowed by a Focke-Wulf, four-engine reconnaissance aircraft, which was working in co-operation with the U-Boats. A signal came through that *"Twenty five U-Boats operating in a pack were expected to attack us, so be on the alert"*. They tried their hardest to get through and managed it on Sunday, 31 October, at 8am, when in broad daylight the Norwegian cargo vessel *S.S. Hallfried* was hit and sunk within the space of fifteen seconds.

It was unbelievable the speed at which she sank, but we learned afterwards she was carrying a cargo of iron ore from West Africa, so this could have accounted for it. The only hindrance after this was being shadowed by a Blohm & Voss six-engine bomber, but we had a Liberator escorting us which soon saw him off. We arrived in England again on 6 November, but after a short leave we were on our way again, this time our destination was Sicily.

By Christmas we were off Pantalleria and landed at Augusta on Boxing Day, but only stayed there for a few hours before going on to Siracuse. Our Christmas was very poor and so was Siracuse. There was plenty of a Biblical historical interest there, such as the cathedral, the amphitheatre and the catacombs, all meeting places for the early Christians about the time of Saint Paul. It offered nothing in the way of entertainment and nothing could be bought except nuts, fruit and cheap wines. The enemy paid occasional sorties over the area but did not cause any trouble. The invasion by the Allies was going well and there was fierce fighting at Casino.

New Year's Day 1944 came and went but we did not celebrate, it was just another tedious, boring day as far as we were concerned. Some of the 8th Army soldiers who were unloading our ship invited us to their camp and we had a few get-togethers before we left on 10 January for Algiers to await further orders. I began to despair and wondered if I should ever rid myself of the Med and the Middle East Campaign. I did not mind as long as I was visiting new places that were interesting, but most of them were not.

We called at Gibraltar again, but I found this to be very disappointing the first time. Casablanca was our next call but I was also glad when we left on 27 January, not knowing until we had been at sea for a day that we were bound for New York.

This news was a tonic for me. For four years I had hoped that one day I would go to America and now I was actually on my way, hoping and praying that nothing untoward would happen to stop us. Nothing did and we arrived safely on 14 February.

Albert Johns

Scene Six – New York and America at Last!

New York, in the grip of a bad winter, did not look very inviting from the sea. That famous skyline lost some of its appeal as the sleet and snow fell, but we all knew of the bright lights in and around Broadway and Times Square, so our main aim was to get shore leave as soon as possible and go to see it all for ourselves. It had always looked so good in the movies.

With no lengthy duties to do whilst we were in port we had lots of time to explore this exciting city. There were so many places of entertainment that we were never at a loss for where to go or what to do. The U.S.O. (United Service Organizations) Club at 99 Park Lane had the details of every kind of show, sporting event and places of interest for Allied Servicemen who wished to avail themselves of these opportunities.

Lists of American families wishing to open their homes were on hand. I was delighted about this and went to spend a weekend with a Doctor, his wife and three teenage daughters in White Plains on the outskirts of New York. It was an education to see how the other half lives. It was like the movie "Three Smart Girls Grow Up" with Deanna Durbin.

I recall the first show I ever saw was at Radio City centre, a 50/50 stage and film show. The latter was the English classic "Jane Eyre" with Joan Fontaine and Orson Welles.

On the stage was Martha Raye, a famous comedienne, along with the famous dancing troupe, The Rockettes. It was a fabulous experience. A young Frank Sinatra was the latest singing sensation of the day and screaming young Bobby-soxers, as they were called, were the craze.

The latest musical on Broadway was "Oklahoma", which had been running for six months and playing to packed houses. It was impossible to get a ticket to see this, may I add. I knew all the lovely tunes long before the show came to the U.K. The cast of the show were frequent visitors to the stage door canteen. It was a popular haunt and I used to pop in most days. There was always one star or another making a public appearance. I saw Celeste Holme, Helen Hayes, Ralph Bellamy and Bette Davis, to name a few. I enjoyed a wonderful production of "The Merry Widow" with Jan Kiepura and Wilma Spence, and also many plays and variety shows too numerous to mention.

When I found time to return to the *Commerce*, I learned she was to undergo extensive changes so we could be in New York for some considerable time. This pleased me immensely but when I was told what they were and why, I wasn't so keen. They were fitting her out to carry 400 mules to India. That meant a return to the Mediterranean, Suez Canal and Red Sea again.

I took ill with a very bad attack of the 'flu and tonsillitis and had to go into hospital in Brooklyn Navy Yard. As I improved I was drafted on to the *H.M.S. Saker*, having been discharged from the *Commerce* to await a new posting when I was better.

After my period of hospitalisation I was given a short leave to recuperate. I knew my wife had relations at Lowell, near Boston, Massachusetts, so I made arrangements to go up and see them for a few days. They made me very welcome and gave me a lovely time, but my orders were to be back by 28 March for my next draft down to Baltimore to pick up my new ship which was the *S.S. Samspelga*.

She was new all right, brand new! Direct from the builder's yard, but with no guarantee that she would stay afloat forever. Anyway, conditions were more spacious for everyone than before and the crew had been sent out from Newcastle upon Tyne to join her there for her maiden voyage. But first of all we had to go to New York to load.

Albert Johns

Scene Seven – Back to the Mediterranean and Home

We returned to Naples, then did the same run again, this time with the American Red Cross Hospital Division. After they had disembarked we made our way to Leghorn (Livorno), in Italy, which was only seventy five miles from where the action was still raging in northern Italy, so it was action stations all the time. The weather was atrocious with constant heavy rain for days on end. We hoped that it would improve by the time we returned to Naples, but it got worse. We lay in Naples harbour for eight days before being told to proceed to Gibraltar. On the journey we had engine trouble so we were detained longer than anticipated. We spent Christmas on the Rock, but set sail for the U.K. on 31 December.

And so New Year's Day 1945 dawned. I had packed a lot into these last few years. What would this New Year bring, I wondered? It was not yet the end of my service life, but it was good to be going home, if only for a short while. The last assignment had kept me away from these shores for almost eighteen months. We took on a cargo of oil and made our way home.

I was demobbed from *H.M.S. Flying Fox* in Bristol. It saddens me, when I think that after all these years of rock and tempest, fire and foe that I was up the Persian Gulf when V.E. Day was being celebrated in Britain on 8 May 1945. Needless to say we enjoyed our own celebrations before we left there.

Albert Johns

ACT THREE – THE THEATRE YEARS – 1945 ONWARDS

COMPILED AND EDITED BY MURRAY AND GRAHAM JOHNS

In the foreword, we made a statement that Albert, in hindsight, did perhaps have one regret, namely that he did not take the gamble of turning professional and try to make a life on the stage. Maybe when you have read Albert's own words, taken from a personal tape recording of a rehearsal for a lecture he was practising to deliver (we think this would have been in around 1986), and viewed some of the accolades he received, you'll have your own views.

Photograph of Albert used by the Theatre

Albert's Narrative

My sweeping statement was "*I could've done better myself*", or as they say in Basford where I come from, "*I coulda done better me sen*". I said this to John Baggaley (a personal friend through the theatre who was an excellent set designer and spent many productive years with the Bairnswear Players). After going with him to a coffee morning where we were to be given a talk by three prominent panto stars who were appearing at Nottingham's Theatre Royal that season, I was dreadfully disappointed and sensed that many of the people there were too.

The three celebrities in question were the Dame, the Principal Boy and the Demon King. We really expected something more exciting, something better and there always seems to be something missing when you meet the stars. Is it their inability to talk off the cuff and to ad-lib, so to speak? Or is it because they cannot communicate, and relate to people, when they are out of character and have to rely on scripts, which they have to learn thoroughly in their line of business?

I don't suppose we shall ever know. Anyway, they did their best but was that good enough? Personally I didn't think so, and I felt that those people who had turned out on that cold January morning expected something different. It was a bit of an anti-climax, if you see what I mean.

It is with sadness that we who live in the Basford area have all watched the demolition of the Bairnswear factory on Perry Road, Basford – a case of legalised vandalism if ever I saw one – and it has been replaced by yet another Do-It-Yourself outlet. Bairnswear had a special place in my heart. Not only did my wife and I, and several members of our family, work there for many years, but it was there, along with others, that I helped to found the Bairnswear Players.

We started in a very humble fashion but very quickly branched out into three act dramas and comedies, which were all very well received by eager audiences. We naturally disbanded at the outbreak of the Second World War but, when we returned after the hostilities were over, Mr Sidney Shephard (the founder and Managing Director of Bairnswear) decided to alter the stage for us. He was a most likeable, friendly and helpful employer and, as a result of his added support and commitment, we became more adventurous and staged bigger and better productions. These included Old Time Music Hall and the hit musicals of the day such as "The Boyfriend", "South Pacific", "Call Me Madam", "Love From Judy", "Guys and Dolls" and the ever-popular "No, No Nanette".

However, it was the introduction of the annual Bairnswear Pantomimes which proved to a major success and became a must for many families. They were really planned for the family and our audiences told us so too! There was no smut, no filth and we did not do anything or say anything that you couldn't say, or do, in front of your old maiden aunt.

I do remember, quite vividly, our first effort at pantomime. It was "Aladdin", a good choice with so much scope, a lovely story line and such opportunity for comedy. The good and bad would each play their part before they all ended up happily ever after at the final curtain. It was a good effort and so our appetites were whetted for this exciting and very rewarding facet of the theatre.

We grew in strength as time went on and we quickly assembled an understanding of pantomime, and its ongoing possibilities, from A to Z. For instance, we were fortunate enough to have John Baggaley as our Set Designer and his gorgeous scenery graced all our productions. Reg Messenger was brilliant at script writing and Geoffrey Spittal was an exceptionally talented Musical Director who had the patience of Job. My contribution was a relentless search for comedy material, simple laugh lines and throwaway gags of which I hope to tell you a few later on. We all agreed that pantomime is glitter, glamour and real escapist entertainment where good always triumphs over evil and "All's well that ends well" as the Bard so rightly put it.

I must admit that I knew very little about pantomime before "Aladdin" as I cannot ever recall seeing one when I was a child. I'd ensure that when my son was able to sit and enjoy this kind of entertainment that we would go. The first one we saw as a family was "Red Riding

Hood" with Julie Andrews in the title role. Tony Hancock was Idle Jack and there was a fellow there named Tony Heaton who played the Dame. This fellow literally had me rolling in the aisles. He was *so* funny and I found that I was so impressed, I remember saying to myself as I sat there, *"Ooh, I'd love to do that!"* I'd love to make people laugh as heartily and as happily as I did that afternoon matinee. I never dreamed that one day I would, and did, for fifteen consecutive years at Bairnswear.

When auditions were held for our first pantomime, "Aladdin", I put in for the Widow Twankey part and I landed it. The rehearsals were a lot of fun but when it came to the opening night I think I died a thousand deaths as I waited to go on for my big scene which is, as you probably know, Widow Twankey's laundry. Prior to setting foot on the stage, however, I switched my apron from front to back. Why I did this I shall never know but I had seen the Andrews Liver Salt advert which was on all the placards around that time, where the old man was packing his case ready to go on holiday and his liver salts were in his back pocket. He was seen scratching his head and underneath it said *"I must have left it behind"*. So I put my box of wash powder in my apron pocket and it was then that I had my gag too.

This proved to be a priceless move for me as, after doing this, I went on the stage and said *"Oh dear I am in a tizzy this morning. I've got lots of work to do and I can't get started no-how. I put my wash powder down somewhere and I just can't find it! If you should see it anywhere, kids, please shout up and let me know."*

Of course, nobody answered, but as I turned round and faced upstage a little voice in the audience said, *"It's in your pocket."* I said, *"What did you say, love?"* and the voice replied *"It's in your pocket."* I said, *"I'm very sorry, duck, but I can't hear you. You see, the older I get, the harder of hearing I get too! You'll just have to shout really loud, now what did you say?"* and all the children shouted at the top of their voices *"It's in your pocket! It's in your pocket!"* I said, *"Oh, bless you. I wish you were all mine. Here, pass me my handbag Wishy Washy and let me give 'em all a copper."* That chorus of voices started me off on my Dame career which was to last for a long, long time and I was never ever afraid of playing the part after that.

The Christmas before last, in 1984, I played the Dame once again in the production of "Cinderella" at the ripe old age of 68. Now that's not bad is it? You know, those children will never know what they did for me on that opening night.

It's dame fame

POSTPHOTO H3570 · Picture by DAVID BAIRD

THERE'S nothing like a dame — so goes the song from *South Pacific*. And that's just what 68-year-old Albert Johns has to say at the start of the pantomime season.

For Albert — pictured showing off his song-and-dance routine at a Curtius Salon coffee morning at Nottingham's New Mechanics' Institute — is a dame specialist.

He first became interested in the theatre in 1937 and started in pantomime three years later. Next week Albert is the baroness in the Co-op Arts Theatre production of *Cinderella*.

His longest stage run was with the Bairnswear Players, with whom he played dame for 15 consecutive years.

Albert, of Perry Road, Basford, said: "I have played all the major dame roles. I really enjoy it as it certainly keeps you feeling young!"

Albert on the Secret of Youth (Courtesy of the Nottingham Post)

I got to know afterwards that we had invited forty deprived children from the Children's Home on Hartley Road in Radford. Not only was it a night to remember for me but it was a red letter night for them too. I recall some years afterwards, when I was going about my work in the Winding Room at Bairnswear, a young lady came up to me and said, "*Mr. Johns, you don't know me, but I was in charge of all those children who came to your opening performance of "Aladdin". We did enjoy it.*" I said, "*And so did I, dear.*" My thanks will always go out to those kids. I shall never ever play to such a good audience as I did that night, my opening night.

CLOSE-UP

"**D**RAMATICS have always been a serious business to me," says Albert Johns, the man who is now splitting his audiences' sides with his performance as "the Dame" in the Bairns-Wear Players' pantomime "Cinderella."

A member of this group for 23 years, he says he has always maintained that if you wish to draw audiences to live theatre and charge them half-a-crown you must give them five bobs' worth in return.

Albert speaks for a group who has always done this, and attendance at all their shows has proved it to be a very wise policy.

Although the greatest part of Albert Johns' "stage life" has been spent in the service of the Bairns-Wear Players, he has appeared with other groups as well — the 1949 pageant and the last two Rotary revues for example— but he misses the intimacy between stage and "stalls" which is always so characteristic of shows in Perry-road.

His favourite roles are all in comedy, but he had mixed feelings when first asked to play a pantomime Dame.

It was in "Aladdin" and the first audience who saw him in this part were nearly all children.

But they put him at his ease, and ever since then he has thoroughly enjoyed this role and I'm sure gets as much kick out of it as his audiences do.

Local Newspaper Article (Source Unknown)

Planning all of our pantomimes began as early as June of the previous year. We would meet on lovely summer evenings in my garden, planning what we should be presenting to you, the public, the following January. "Cinderella", "Aladdin", "Jack and the Beanstalk" and "Dick Whittington" always dwell on the same storyline, but when you come to "Red Riding Hood" or "Humpty Dumpty", the story needs a lot of building up and a lot of padding. This meant we had to put our heads together and do a lot of thinking for some new, entertaining ideas. Thankfully we did it and I'm glad to say we were always crowned with success.

For spectacle, the best pantomime is "Cinderella", but the most popular is "Mother Goose" – this is my favourite too and I've enjoyed playing in it on three occasions. "Mother Goose" is to pantomime what "Hedda Gabler" and "Hamlet" are to legitimate theatre. My contribution to the script, as I've said before, was always an everlasting search for comedy material – gags, funny sayings and situations – simple throwaway gags like the Dame saying to Idle Jack, "'Ere! Why don't you grow up, stupid!" to which he replied, "I did grow up stupid!" And then there was another one where Idle Jack said, "I heard somebody knocking so I got up and opened the door in my pyjamas." To which the Dame replied, "Ooh, what a funny place to have a door!"

I used to listen to people like yourselves talking and watch all your movements and really we are all very funny in our off moments aren't we? Some of us are more funny than others but many people are unconscious comedians in their own right aren't they? I still find myself doing this sort of thing today you know, and saying to myself, "That would go down well in pantomime." For instance, there were two ladies on the bus in Nottingham, and one was a visitor to the city, and the other lady said, "Are you enjoying your stay in the city then?" to which she replied, "Yes! Yes! Very much, but it's very cosmopolitan isn't it? I mean, aren't there a lot of Chinese here?" Amazed, the local lady said, "Well I've never noticed, there's only those who keep the takeaways and the restaurants." The visitor replied, "Ooh, there are. Almost everyone you meet says 'Ooohwashyweeanywonoohwashywearsen?', now if that isn't Chinese I don't know what is!"

To those of you unfamiliar with the East Midlands dialect and pronunciation, this loosely means, "Was she with anyone or was she by herself?"

Dialects play a big part in our lives and they are really wonderful aren't they? I remember a young girl coming to work at Bairnswear fresh from school and no matter what she said, she would always finish up the conversation by saying "Eh, shurrup!" I thought to myself, "What a lovely catchphrase to use in panto whenever an opportunity arises!" and it did more often than not. I used it on many occasions to great advantage. "Eh, shurrup!" was to me, what "Nice to see you, to see you nice!" is to Bruce Forsyth, which he used again in "Cinderella" the other year.

I am sure that we all agree that pantomime is really for children but it's good to know that even at our age we enjoy the simple things in life. I mean, we're all children at heart, aren't we? After a hard day's work at the factory, I would go home absolutely exhausted and I would say to myself, "Gosh, I'm so tired, I don't know how I'll get through the show tonight." But as soon as I got into my costume, and had my wig and makeup put on, I was transformed. I was transported into the realms of fantasy where troubles vanish with a wave of a magic wand and for two-and-a-half to three hours I was away from all my worldly worries and took my audiences along with me.

And children are always good to entertain, aren't they? They readily get into the spirit of it all, but you can't fool them. Impress them? Yes! I have two very amusing incidents which always come to my mind to prove this. When we did "The Sleeping Beauty", the Major Domo was played as a poor, doddering old man – it was written that way of course – I played the Queen who was not amused by his shortcomings and I made it known in my chatter about him. I would say such things as "*I don't know what I'm going to do with him, I don't really! He's getting past it you know, that's his trouble! I shall have to get rid of him! He's getting far too old for the job! He's got one foot in the grave already! You know he must be 103 if he's a day! One day I'll drop a bit of something in his tea and put him out of his misery!*" A lady saw me three days after seeing the show, she said how much they'd enjoyed it all but she said how angry her nine-year-old daughter was at the way I'd treated the old man and the awful things I'd said to him. She really took all I'd said to heart and for a while, you know, I lost a fan through being far too realistic. I'm glad to say I got her back when we decided to do "Robinson Crusoe" the following year.

After doing so many pantos, you get a bit stuck for ideas on how to bring on the Dame for her first entrance. I've come on in laundry baskets, on roller skates or scooters and, in "Ali Baba", I was the fifth slave from the left in the auction market in Old Baghdad.

The entrance which impressed one of the children most was when I was in a later version of "Aladdin" and I made my first entrance from the back of the hall as if I was a patron who was coming in late. There was a competition going on, on the stage, and it went something like this. I said:

"*Oh, has it started?*"

"*Yes, Madam, would you kindly sit down?*"

"*Yes, but you're a bit early aren't you? I mean, it says 7:30 on my ticket…Ooh, now, oh, no it don't. It says 7:15, now I am sorry, I am sorry now. Carry on.*"

"*Thank you, Madam.*"

"How far have you got then? Could you go back to the beginning cos I always have to tell him all about it when I get home you know?"

"Madam, we're running a singing competition! Would you care to join in?"

"Me? No thank you! I can't sing! I don't know though, did you say I might get a prize?"

"Well, yes Madam, there are three prizes and we need three contestants. Do go up and have a go!"

So I went up on stage and the contest began, the first singer did her number and got a parcel which she asked to unwrap, revealing a huge jug. The second lady sang and her parcel contained a washbasin. After my song, I was presented with a third parcel. The audience automatically guessed what it was – what they assumed it was, shall I say (so did I) – and I said *"I don't want it! I know what it is! We've got one anyway! As a matter of fact, we've got three, we've got one in each bedroom!"*

He said, *"I don't think you have, Madam. Do open it up and let everyone see."* I did so and it was a lovely goldfish bowl rather than the gazunder everyone was expecting. I said, *"Ooh, what a lovely goldfish bowl! That's fooled you, hasn't it?"* and I left the stage. The reason for me relating this incident is to make a point about how you create the illusion in the children's minds and when they leave the theatre they still think of you as the character you played.

Someone said to me that after every show you should remove your wig, to which I replied, *"No way! Am I going to spoil it for the children before they go home?"* Why spoil it? Pantomime is not soldiers in skirts or one of those revue type of shows that were doing the rounds about that time.

Several photos of Albert in Dame Costume, with John Slater as Wishy Washy and Barbara Biddulph as Aladdin.

I must tell you this little story and it proved to me that I was right. My boss at Bairnswear came to me one Monday morning in June as soon as he arrived at work. He said, *"Albert, I must tell you this as it seemed so funny after six months. My young son, Timothy, came into our bedroom early yesterday morning. He was hardly awake and neither were we but the first thing he said was 'Daddy, that lady who came in late at the pantomime, she was funny wasn't she?'"* He said, *"You must've made a good impression on him for him to remember after all that time."* I said, *"I'm glad I did."* It just proved my point so the wig always stays on until the audiences have left the theatre. I say let them go home still in this land of make-believe and stay there as long as they can. After all, the outside world is no joy is it?

How fortunate we were at Bairnswear and many of us never did appreciate it until it folded and we decided to join other societies. As a matter of fact, we were feather-bedded with no restriction on the financial side, within reason of course. As long as the shows were a success and drew the crowds, it was considered to be a good investment by the management and the Bairnswear sports club, to whom we were eternally grateful.

The costumes, for instance, were all hired from theatrical agencies. I recall once I had sixteen gorgeous outfits and five different wigs when I played in "Mother Goose". Nelly Smith (the theatre outfitter on Mansfield Road) always did us proud and the ladies in her workroom always had a surprise dress made especially for me to wear for the very first time. Ruby Stokes, who has just passed away at the age of 94, and her team always looked forward to the Saturday morning when I would go down and model it for them in that upper room. They were such happy days. I have such happy memories of it all.

With so many costume changes to make throughout the show and some very quick ones at that; within half a page of dialogue I had to get into these costumes quicker than quick, so to speak. I'm pleased to say that I had the help of two very dear ladies who stood by me and were always there as I came off the stage. They were so reliable and knew just what I needed. In short, they were as word-perfect off the stage as I had to be on it.

Makeup was in the hands of another old friend, Elsie Jackson. When I was poor and being turned out of my cottage by the wicked squire, believe me, I *looked* poor and haggard. Elsie would see to that! But when good fortune struck and the goose laid the golden eggs and I wished for wealth and beauty, I was transformed by Elsie, who was a master of the art of makeup.

The Bairnswear stage was wide and narrow, rather like a cinemascope effect. The measurements were twenty-two feet across, nine feet high and ten feet in depth from the footlights to the back wall, which meant there was very little wing space, if any, I might add. The effects created by John Baggaley, who knew every inch of this stage and its possibilities, were fantastic. Often people would ask to see backstage and they were amazed at the lack of space we had despite the alterations that had already been made. Remember we were still a factory and had certain industrial regulations we had to comply with.

When we got established, our regular customers always looked forward to the special spot in pantomime which Reg and I did. It was considered to be the highlight of the show. Reg, who was not only a brilliant scriptwriter but also a comedian in his own right, was a perfect stooge on these occasions. We always planned a special spot around something that was popular or topical at that particular time.

I think the best one that we ever did was the skit on the BBC's "Come Dancing". The idea was that we should be a couple of champion ballroom dancers engaged in winning the challenge cup. In essence we would watch others perform and pass humorous comments about their efforts before delivering our award winning performance and taking the accolades of everyone around us.

Another important factor was the choice of songs for the pantomime. Throughout the year we would search for songs which would be appropriate for the show. We made sure that our songs would continue to tell the story. We never featured any of the songs that featured on "Top of the Pops". Our songs had to be pleasing to the ear as our costumes and scenery had to be pleasing to the eye.

The audience participation song, which you as the public are always asked to join in, was always a special choice. Geoffrey Spittal wrote some special ones and we used some good oldies too including "Do-Re-Mi", "The Happiness Tree", "Hi-Ho!", "Chick, Chick, Chick, Chick, Chicken!" and "I Lift Up My Finger" to name but a few. And in "Robinson Crusoe", when we taught Man Friday to talk, we sang "The Alphabet Song". You know the one, *"A, you're adorable, B, you're so beautiful, C, you're a cutie full of charms"* … and it fitted so well into the story.

What would your personal choice be? "Pack Up Your Troubles", "Oh What a Beautiful Morning" or perhaps it would be "Edelweiss"? The list is endless but it had to be a song which gave everyone the chance to let their hair down and have a good sing! Those conducting the sing-along would provide much needed encouragement and the dialogue would be along the lines of "*... come on it will do you all a world of good, you know it will. You'll feel twenty years younger before you leave here today!*" The important thing for us, as the cast, was to ensure that everyone left the auditorium with a smile on their face!

Before I close you may be interested to know some historical facts relating to the role of Pantomime Dame. Men played the part of women long before the advent of pantomime. The Greeks, the Romans and the Elizabethans all expected the female roles to be taken by men. Even in the theatrically liberated eighteenth century, some actresses preferred to see their male colleagues playing the part of older and more ludicrous women in high comedy and farce. The tradition of having men impersonate women on stage survived into the era of pantomime.

The great clown, Joseph Grimaldi, for instance, played Queen Ronabellyana in "Harlequin and the Red Dwarf" at Covent Garden in 1812. But the Dame as we know her today did not become established until the 1860s onwards when the music hall performers began to appear regularly in pantomimes. It was then that the glorious comedy potential of Dick Whittington's cook, Martha, the Sleeping Beauty's mother, Mrs. Crusoe, Dame Durden and all the rest were fully realised.

Pantomime would not be pantomime without the Dame. Can you imagine "Cinderella" without the Ugly Sisters? "Jack and the Beanstalk" without Dame Trott? "Aladdin" without Widow Twankey? It would be like Christmas without Santa Claus. A contradiction in terms and a very, very dreary one at that.

And now, following that little insight into the history books, I feel I must tell you some amusing incidents which I encountered as I studied people to enable me to form my Dame character.

There are two old dears who regularly go to the Co-Operative Arts Theatre, but dare not stay until the end because of the muggings which are going on these days. They get restless at about 9:30 and get up to go, but they don't do it quietly, far from it! You can hear them say in a loud voice to those around them, "*We're going now, Lizzie, to catch us buses. Now let us know how it finishes when we see you at bingo tomorrow.*" In essence they've no thought for the audience who may be engrossed in some stark drama or complicated plot, or for the poor performer who is battling hard to concentrate on stage.

A friend of mine said that he could hardly believe his ears as he walked on stage in one show. He had not uttered a word before he heard an old dear on the front row say in a loud voice, "*Here's him you don't like, Ada.*" He felt so demoralised at the time but saw the funny side of it when he had time to think about it later on in the dressing room. We are a funny lot aren't we? We shall always survive whilst we are able to have a good laugh at ourselves.

I think one of the funniest things that I've ever heard was when a friend of mine and his wife took their two small children to a pantomime at the Royal. When they got home, Grandpa was there waiting to hear all about it. He said to the youngest one, "*And what did you like best about the pantomime?*" to which the little child replied, "*The seats Grandpa! They pop up and down!*"

They always say that, wherever you are in the world, you never know who you're going to meet up with, though the instance I'm going to quote here was very close to home, literally! Ever since I first trod the boards, when I was at the National School at Hucknall, I played the back end of a donkey. I know a lot of people write this when they write their memoirs but with me it was true!

One day I was speaking about my experiences in pantomime to the Byron Ladies in Hucknall (remember that I was born there in 1916). The venue was the Church Hall on Ogle Street, very close to where I was born on Annesley Road.

I said how glad I was to be back in that building after in excess of forty years. I was thrilled because, as I said to those present, I actually started my career on that stage. I related the incident of being the back end of a donkey, and a lady on the front row said "*I know you were, because I was the front end.*" I said, "*You really was?*" and she said, "*Yes, I'm Frances Reedon. You used to sit next to me at school.*" And then of course, everyone else in the audience said "*Yes, and I know you.*" It went on like that.

I've always been very serious about the theatre. There's never been any half measures with me at all. I used to give coaching at the Church Hall and I always remember one little girl singing a lullaby to her dolly, and she was doing it very well indeed. Then she looked down at her dolly sympathetically, stopped and said, "*Ooh, its eyes have dropped out!*" I had to laugh when it happened but when I got her in the dressing room I said, "*You oughtn't to say that, you ought to carry on, you carry on regardless of what happens.*"

Anyway, thank you very much for sharing my memories. I do hope you've enjoyed your stroll with me down my Memory Lane and I've brought back some fond memories for you, and of all your childhood visits to the theatre and, in particular, the magical, escapist world of pantomime. God bless you all.

A Fine Dame

I hear splendid reports on the show "One Eve in Midsummer" which pupils of the Morrison School of Dancing are performing at the Co-operative Arts Theatre. It should furnish quite handsome proceeds for the Royal Midland Institution for the Blind by the time the last performance is given tomorrow night. Among the guest artists playing character roles in this charming fantasy is Albert Johns, shown above with other members of the cast in his familiar disguise as a kind of pantomime "dame," a part in which he always excels.

Praise for Albert (Source Unknown)

***

The following is an article first published in 2000 (Courtesy of the Nottingham Post):

Smell of greasepaint

THERE is nothing like a dame, and young at heart senior citizen Albert Johns has been reflecting on his 60-year involvement in amateur theatre and the times when he was regarded as "one of the best pantomime dames in the business".

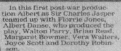

The *Post*'s April Bygones publication brought back many happy memories for Albert, 84, and while he found the stories, pictures and anecdotes in its pages "fascinating", he has expressed his disappointment that there was no mention of his beloved Bairnswear Players.

From an early age, Albert, the son of a miner and a product of Hucknall National School, influenced by stars such as Harry Lauder, Arthur Lucan (Old Mother Riley) and George Formby, fancied his chances as a stage performer.

"I used to love the smell of the greasepaint, the dressing up and taking centre stage in front of an audience.

"I used to star in school plays and pantomimes and was described as a natural," enthused Albert.

"But before very long I found myself following in father's footsteps and doing something completely different to what I really wanted and that was working down the pit.

"My dreams of becoming a thespian went right out of the window until one day opportunity knocked and I was offered employment as a knitter at Bairnswear in Perry Road.

"I never looked back and in 1934 was among a small group of troupers who helped to form the Bairnswear Players which went on to become a tour de force in amateur theatre circles," said Albert.

The Bairnswear Players' first productions were the three act plays *Miss Smith*, in which Tom Hebb starred as Lord Peter Wimsey and Albert Johns as the Rev Simon Goodacre, *Busman's Honeymoon* and *Busman's Holiday* in which Tom and Albert played the same characters.

Performances were staged in the packed factory ballroom where audiences were largely made up of employees who obviously enjoyed seeing their work colleagues in their dramatic guises.

Albert was just starting to relish his new found fame as one of Bairnswear's star performers when the Second World War reared its ugly head and the drama group's activities were suspended.

In no time at all Albert found himself swapping theatrical garb for that of a different kind — Royal Navy uniform.

For five years Albert, a veteran of the Tobruk Campaign, served as a gunner in the Merchant Navy aboard the *Manchester Commerce*, *SS Samois* and *SS Scythia*.

Relieved to have arrived home (which was Rockford Road, Basford, just a stone's throw away from his place of work) in one piece, Albert and the Bairnswear Players resumed activities in 1946 with a production of Emlyn Williams' classic ghost story *A Murder Has Been Arranged*.

In this first post-war production Albert as Sir Charles Jasper teamed up with Florrie Jones, Albert Danse, who produced the play, Walton Parry, Brian Read, Margaret Bowmer, Vera Wolters, Joyce Scott and Dorothy Robinson.

In January 1952, Albert fulfilled a personal ambition by taking on the role of Widow Twankey in the group's first pantomime *Aladdin*, which featured Kenneth Young as Abanazar, Johnnie Shooter (Wishy Washy) and Dorothy Robinson in the title role.

The show was produced and directed by Reg Messenger and marked the first use of a newly extended stage, work that had been authorised by Bairnswear then chairman and managing director Sidney Shephard.

Playing the Dame became Albert's forte and his reputation in amateur theatre circles was second to none. For more than 30 years he delighted audiences with his antics in pantomime and upon the demise of the Bairnswear Players he switched his allegiance to the Co-operative Arts Theatre.

"We had some great times on the Bairnswear stage and I was regarded as 'Mr Theatre' by my peers," said Albert.

"The 1970s marked the end of an era, the firm was taken over by Courtaulds and the building was later demolished to make way for W. H. Smith's Focus Do-It-All store.

Recently Albert, who is now a resident of Sycamore House, a residential home run by the Abbeyfield Nottingham Society, attended an old time music hall production being staged by the Co-op Arts Theatre team.

Compering the show was Ken Godfrey who goes back a long way with Albert. "We starred together in numerous productions for the Co-op Arts Theatre.

"One that sticks out more than most was the pantomime *Mother Goose* which was staged in 1982," said Albert.

"Ken took on the title role and I played another dame, a character named Mercedes. Together we were dynamite and received standing ovations."

In a fitting tribute to a great amateur performer Mr Godfrey described Albert as "a super trouper".

"He lit up the stage, always had a wonderful rapport with his audiences and had that one vital ingredient which made him an exceptional talent — star quality!"

AFTERWORD

WITH CONTRIBUTIONS FROM GRAHAM, MURRAY & STEVE JOHNS

Albert & Ethel with Steve, Murray and Graham

My Grandpa – By Graham Johns

When I first had the idea of compiling and publishing Grandpa's memoirs as a book (something I hope he'd be thrilled about), having read them for the first time properly around six months prior, I realised how little I really knew him. At the time I conceived the idea, it was already fourteen years since his death in 2004.

I wasn't sure how to feel about this personal revelation of how little I knew my own grandparent. It's not that he was a quiet or reserved man, far from it, as he always seemed full of life and I guess his life in amateur theatre often meant that he could always turn on a show as and when required. Perhaps my lack of knowledge speaks more about me or about children in general and a lack of attention paid to important family relationships which help shape you as a person. If you can truly remember your grandparent, having taken the time to know them properly as an adult, I think you are quite fortunate. It does make me wonder how well we really know anyone though. People largely are just busy going about their lives and maybe telling us about things that mean something to them – if they remember to do so.

As children, my younger brother Steve and I didn't see him or Grandma that often. Indeed the first things that I can recall easily seem quite negative at face value. I can remember Grandma having more than one stroke in her later years and largely being restricted to a life switching between a chair and bed – with Grandpa caring for her largely by himself. I guess I can conclude from this what a caring and kind man he was – I certainly never heard him complain, and nor did I ever hear Grandma complain. Mum always says he is the kindest man she has ever met so maybe my recollection is fair. They must have found life hard at times but this was never mentioned in my presence.

Grandma still liked an occasional cigarette until the end of her life but she never smoked when the grandchildren visited because she knew we didn't like the smell. It's strange given how much time she must've spent in the house that I really don't recall a smell of smoke associated with her at all.

Oddly, I remember that their house always seemed to be spotless, that they always had a top-loading washing machine that I'd never seen anywhere else, and the slowest (and perhaps most effective) flushing toilet I've ever seen to this day – for some bizarre reason it used to fill up from underneath and push things up before sucking them down – anyway, I digress.

What about more positive memories?

Well, I always enjoyed Grandma's custard…it was the thinnest custard I've ever had! Just like sweet, creamy, yellowy water in many ways!

Grandpa always used to call my brother and I "*Manny*"...I'm told that was reserved for when someone was acting up a bit. Perhaps it related to manners. It always made us laugh though in the way he said it. I like to think some of the values I carry to this day were taught by him, I certainly value manners and courtesy in myself and others. I think he first ensured that, as children, we got to go to see a pantomime and were exposed to theatre as this was where his passion lay. I hope that he'd be totally overjoyed that I've now published multiple books, including his memoirs.

I can vaguely recall seeing a pantomime with Barbara Windsor in the title role in "Aladdin", in Nottingham, when young. I imagine some of this would be down to him. We saw films such as "Who Framed Roger Rabbit?" and "Back to the Future 2" together. We also often visited a small village called Papplewick, near Nottingham, for Sunday lunch and would go for walks at Wollaton Park. They used to give us pocket money every year until we were in our late teens in lieu of a visit to Goose Fair, an annual funfair held in Nottingham, whether we went to the fair or not. I've a feeling I may only have been a few times at most.

When I was a little older, I was told he once dressed up as Santa Claus and, having been to see him, I commented that he looked just like Grandpa. It makes me wonder how many of the memories we have from our childhood are perhaps planted there by the things your parents tell you about your younger years. Whatever the case, I enjoyed visiting them and I think they used to perhaps spoil us a bit because we didn't see them every week. Grandpa could make things fun just with a look or a smile or a phrase, and that is a rare gift. I'd like to think I've inherited a bit of his artistic and comedic talent!

Albert as Santa with Steve and Graham on his Knees

I seem to think he was a humble man, not prone to bragging, but I can recall one thing he was truly proud of was his amateur dramatics as a Pantomime Dame. I don't think I ever saw him perform but he did quote of how his performance had once been cited in a newspaper as good enough to bring the house down at Drury Lane. That's quite an achievement for someone who gave himself freely for his art.

Mum told me about how Albert had a terrific sense of humour and was always ready with a comment which would, at the very least, make you smile if not roll about with laughter. He had related many of his war and theatre experiences to her over time, and yet there is so much more than she knew. On recalling his time in theatre, she only once saw him as a Pantomime Dame, during which he did a strip tease on stage, and how he must have had twelve layers of clothing on so it took quite some time. Just when you thought it was the last layer, along came another one. Everyone was in fits of laughter. Another anecdote she told both Steve and I about his humour was relating to his watching Princess Anne riding a horse in the Olympics and commenting that this was stretching a good thing too far...I guess you can judge that in whichever way suits your style of humour.

After my parents divorced we saw Dad once a fortnight on average. Sometimes this would encompass a visit to Nottingham to see my grandparents. Neither Grandpa or Grandma ever drove a car so I don't recall them ever coming to visit us. I'm not sure the divorce really affected the frequency of visits as I think Dad tried to ensure that we still saw them reasonably regularly, and Mum would still take us to visit as she always had a lot of time for her in-laws.

Where I think Grandpa was perhaps unusual was that he actually talked about his experiences in wartime (hence this book), although not to excess like Uncle Albert in "Only Fools and Horses". My Grandad on my Mum's side was also engaged in the conflict, in the Army in North Africa, but never talked about it aside from an occasional joke such as how you needed to run in zig-zags to get away from snakes that could outrun you! Even after reading such works as this memoir and watching increasingly graphic movies, you still can't truly appreciate the horrors they must've witnessed during the Second World War. Grandpa clearly felt that his story was one worth telling.

When I read about his war years now, one thing strikes me more than anything else; if he hadn't avoided those torpedoes then I wouldn't be here today, because Dad was born in 1946 after the war had ended. So in many ways I owe my existence to pure luck. Perhaps we all do and just don't realise it. Grandpa was a religious man so may have proclaimed it an act of God. That's fine too. Either way, it's quite humbling to think that you owe your own existence, at least in part, to something that happened over thirty years before you were born. I'm sure there were other such events in the past of my ancestors that I don't know about but it's amazing nonetheless.

In his later life, Grandpa used to regularly deliver talks about various aspects of his life – which have been used in part to build this book – to nursing homes, the British Legion and Women's Institute, to name a few, all out of the goodness of his heart. Sadly, in his final years, he had to reside in nursing homes in Nottingham and I didn't see him as often as I perhaps could have done due to educational and then work commitments. I have a feeling my parents tried to protect my brother and I a little to try and remember Grandpa as he was, a man who was always full of life and full of fun, despite hardships.

Do I wish I knew him a bit better than I find I now do? Yes, absolutely, but there is nothing I can do about it now except to publish his work as his legacy of a life that made a difference to others; and often that difference was joy and entertainment – given freely. There are no finer words I can write in tribute to Grandpa, and indeed to Grandma who was also almost always there to support him and indeed ourselves.

Dad – By Murray Johns

Albert with a young Murray

I was born in December 1946 and my parents always tried to ensure that I had the opportunities which had not been available to them. This was typical of many who had suffered the deprivation of the 1920s and 1930s and the harrowing experience of the Second World War.

We were not wealthy but Dad and Mum worked hard and were good providers. Neither of them drove so we went everywhere by bus or train and this included a weekly visit, on a Sunday, from our home in Basford to Dad's parents in Hucknall. He considered it important that he maintained regular contact and I should also build a close relationship with them. Grandma Johns was a shrinking violet in many respects while Gilbert was extremely quiet and you struggled to get two words out of him! I have little history regarding my Mum's parents – her mother died (I know not when or where) but I did meet Charles Louis Robinson and her stepmother, Lily, who was only seven years older than her.

You have read how close Dad was to his sister, Annie. After the War she and her husband relocated to Torquay in Devon where she ran a Post Office with her sister-in-law. This meant we often spent our summer holiday in Torquay so we could combine our two week annual break with a visit to see her. We certainly knew our way around that area of Devon.

If we didn't venture to the West Country we invariably spent our Holidays going on day trips organised by Bartons or Skills Coach Tours, taking in sights in the Cotswolds, Leicestershire and Warwickshire. As I got older we used to go away for the Christmas period and we spent many Christmas breaks at the Boston Hotel on Scarborough's North Shore.

You may remember that Dad had little interest in sport but he did everything to foster my interest. Although he disliked football he took me to see both Notts County and Nottingham Forest and, from the age of eight, I was a regular on the terraces of County. To this day I love live sport rather than watching it on television. He instilled into me that "*If it's a team game then there are two teams playing so try to see and appreciate the merits of both participants*". I'd like to think that Graham and Steve share these views.

Dad also disliked gardening and always used to say that if he could have swept the garden at their house with a brush he would've done so!

I represented my school at cricket, rugby, athletics and cross country and, in addition, played for Dad's work's team at cricket. I would like to think that I share, and display, the core values which enriched Mum and Dad's time on earth – honesty, integrity, loyalty, respect for individuals and their possessions, to name a few. However, I did see Dad taken advantage of on far too many occasions so I don't suffer fools gladly. Dad was good with bookkeeping and all things connected with administration and this is certainly something I've always been good at too.

Dad tried to foster my interest in the theatre and I did help out at Bairnswear by assisting behind the scenes with numerous shows with lighting, sound and props and, on rare occasions, helping out in the chorus in crowd scenes – nothing too grandiose though. It definitely wasn't my scene but I did share in Dad's passion and success and agree he was an excellent Pantomime Dame. It never worried me that he was playing the part of the Dame and it was pleasing that he brought enjoyment to so many. What made him so good? Possibly because it was a relief valve from the hardships he had to endure in his early life – like so many theatrical people, he was able to get into character and become someone else for a few hours!

As a consequence of Dad's interest in the theatre, I spent the majority of my leisure time with Mum and we tackled cricket, darts and snooker as well as numerous board games in my early years. This meant I became extremely close to Mum until I left home in 1965, going to Salford University as part of my early career with East Midlands Gas. Mum had no major problems with his time spent at the theatre as it caused no offence to anyone, although there were occasions when she would have to remind him, in a quiet but polite manner that *"he was not on the stage and entertaining now"*, or in other words *"it's your family you're with now, not the paying public"*.

As a result of his theatrical interests, our family social life centred around his fellow thespians and their other halves. It was in essence a happy family and Mum enjoyed the company of the others, many of whom she used to work with.

From 1965 onwards I have never lived in Nottingham (I moved away for employment) and my working life has seen me live in Warwickshire, Leicestershire, North Nottinghamshire, Manchester, South Wales, Cheshire and Derbyshire. Wherever I've lived, I always tried to see Mum and Dad at least once every two weeks and, when the children were younger, to ensure they had regular contact.

Mum and Dad certainly had an impact on Graham and Steve and it's still good to hear them quote some of Dad's stories and anecdotes which have registered with them throughout the years.

It was whilst living in Wales that Mum died and, for the next ten years we saw the rapid decline in Dad's health and well-being. He used to effectively run his own home but was encouraged by some well-meaning friends to sell up and move into residential care. In our opinion he did this far too soon because, within a short space of time, he couldn't even boil a kettle and make a cup of tea. He became totally dependent on the carers and we had to closely monitor where he went on his forays into Nottingham from the care home.

Latterly it was necessary to move him into secure accommodation as it became dangerous for him to venture out on his own. It was a sad end for someone who had seen, and done, so much in his life. It was undoubtedly a full one and, during his time with us, he entertained and provided enjoyment to many people which gave him considerable pleasure and satisfaction.

My wife, Marjorie, and I encouraged Dad to record his thoughts and experiences – he'd talked about doing it for years but never had. We agreed to draft everything for him. Ironically it was his theatre exploits which he struggled with most of all, possibly because Mum wasn't there to drive him on. I hope you have enjoyed reading about his life as much as he used to enjoy bringing enjoyment to others during it.

Grandpa – By Steve Johns

Put simply, the show must go on; and it was always worth an encore.

To epitomise everything he stood for, I remember visiting him on the evening of Christmas Eve 2000, at the nursing home he was residing in. He took great pleasure in going round all the residents introducing us.

In keeping with his stage persona, he'd introduce you and then say something as an aside about the person he'd introduced you to. This ranged from saying that, *"This is Doris (deaf as a bloody post), DORIS, DORIS…THIS IS MY GRANDSON."*

Or perhaps, *"Bert, are you awake? (He probably won't make it to Christmas). Don't get up, Bert."*

He would also introduce you to the staff and make some reference to the fact, *"You wouldn't leave your wallet around that one,"* or something similar.

If you're remembered by how many people turn up at your funeral then he obviously did pretty well. Either that or he died before every other person just to humour himself. After all, you should always leave the audience wanting more.

I remember his fondness for the word *"bugger"* and *"manny"* more than anything else. As a cheeky little lad, I often warranted either or both!

He was a very respectful man, very gentle, but above all a comedy genius. He may well be the first comedian I never knew I knew, probably my first hero, and I had the best seat in the house. I just wish, now that I'm old enough to greater appreciate him, that we could have one last encore.

Albert Johns

ALBERT'S TIMELINE

Significant dates taken from Albert's narrative:

Date	Event
25 March 1916	Albert Edward Johns is born in Hucknall, Nottinghamshire.
1 January 1941	Called to the colours to play his part in the war effort – choosing the Royal Navy.
9 June 1941	Albert weds Ethel Gertrude Robinson.
13 July 1941	Arrives in first foreign country, Freetown, Sierra Leone on the *S.S. Pułaski.*
10 August 1941	Sets sail on *Nieuw Amsterdam* from Durban, South Africa.
24 August 1941	Arrives in Suez.
19 October 1941	Sent on a train to link up with *Gibel Kebir.*
20 October 1941	Leaves base at Alexandria for first mission guarding the *Gibel Kebir* en route to Tobruk.
1 January 1942	Learns he is to be taken off the *Gibel Kebir.*
19 January 1942	Back to Tobruk but this time on *S.S. Manoula.*
26 February 1942	Commissioned to the *S.S. Goviken.*
29 June 1942	*Goviken* is torpedoed off Madagascar and sinks. Albert and others are rescued two days later by the *S.S. Phemius,* which survives a torpedo attack on the following morning.

Date	Event
10 July 1942	Arrives in Cape Town.
13 August 1942	Boards the *S.S. Hindustan* for a journey to the U.K.
23 September 1942	Arrives in Liverpool for thirty days leave.
22 November 1942	Arrives at Algiers.
23 February 1943	Joins *S.S. Manchester Commerce* for journey to U.K.
1 April 1943	Joins convoy heading across Atlantic Ocean to Canada.
2 May 1943	Begins return journey back to U.K. from Saint John, Canada.
22 September 1943	*S.S. Manchester Commerce* arrives in Port Tewfik, Egypt.
14 October 1943	Departs for Algiers.
27 January 1944	Departs Casablanca.
14 February 1944	Arrives in New York.
28 March 1944	Drafted to Baltimore to pick up *S.S. Samspelga*.
8 May 1945	V.E. Day is celebrated, marking the end of the Second World War in Europe. Albert is in the Persian Gulf at the time.
12 May 1994	Ethel dies, aged 86, ending 52 years of marriage to Albert.
26 March 2004	Albert dies, aged 88, a day after his birthday.

SHIPPING LEDGER

The following is a ledger of ships noted in Albert's wartime narrative in chronological order (ships names given as they appear in the narrative):

Ship	Albert's History
H.M.S. Collingwood	Shore-based training unit at Fareham where Albert went for a ten week course in January 1941. Still in use by the Royal Navy.
H.M.S. Excellent	The Royal Navy's Gunnery School, situated in Portsmouth Harbour on Whale Island. Albert attended an eighteen day course in 1941 and scored 87/100.
S.S. Pułaski	Polish vessel Albert boarded in June 1941 for his first trip overseas from Gourock, Scotland, to Durban, South Africa, via Freetown, Sierra Leone.
Empress of Japan & Queen of Bermuda	Troop ships which accompanied the Pułaski as part of the convoy in Albert's first journey from Gourock to Durban.
Nieuw Amsterdam	Luxurious Dutch liner which Albert took from Durban to Suez (Port Tewfik) in August 1941.
Georgic	The burnt out shell of the Georgic liner was observed by Albert as he arrived at Port Tewfik in Egypt.
Gibel Kebir	Albert joined the Gibel Kebir in October 1941 at Alexandria and was aboard during supply runs to Tobruk.
Maria Giovanni	Italian schooner which, along with the Gibel Kebir, served Tobruk with supplies.

Ship	Albert's History
H.M.S. Wolborough	Trawler which accompanied Albert, on the *Gibel Kebir*, as an escort vessel on their run to Tobruk.
Serenitas, Liguria, San Giorgio, Draco & Chantala	Wrecks observed by Albert as they arrived in Tobruk. The *Serenitas, Liguria* and *San Giorgio* were Italian, *Draco and Chantala* British. The *Gibel Kebir* unloaded its cargo by the *Serenitas* to try to disguise them as a wreck.
S.S. Zealand	Made its first supply run in accompanying the *Gibel Kebir* in December 1941.
S.S. Volo	Led the convoy of ships back from Tobruk in December 1941, of which the *Gibel Kebir* was a part. Was hit during the trip with fourteen survivors.
S.S. Manoula	Albert was aboard this vessel on 19 January 1942 for another assault on Tobruk.
H.M.S. Peony	A mine sweeper which accompanied the *Manoula* on its journey to Tobruk in January 1942.
S.S. Goviken	Albert was commissioned to the *Goviken* in February 1942. The ship was torpedoed on 29 June 1942 just off Madagascar, sinking as a result.
S.S. Phemius	British ship which rescued Albert and his crewmates after drifting in a lifeboat after the *Goviken* was sunk. Was torpedoed the following morning but survived the attack.

Ship	Albert's History
H.M.S. Hecla	Albert spent time with crew from the *Hecla* at Worcester, South Africa, after he returned there following his rescue on the *Phemius*.
S.S. Hindustan	Albert joined this vessel on 13 August 1942, taking cotton from Egypt to Liverpool, United Kingdom.
Scythia	Albert was aboard as he returned to action from Liverpool to Algiers in November 1942.
Duchess of York, Letitia, Orontes, Orion, Windsor Castle & Staffordshire	Some of the twenty eight troopships which were part of the convoy, including the *Scythia* on the trip to Algiers.
S.S. Esneh	Albert's friend, Norman Howard, was aboard this ship, running petrol and ammunition to Algeria.
S.S. Merope	Albert's friend, Taffy, was aboard this ship, doing the same run as the *Esneh*.
S.S. Fintra	Frank Bawden and Jimmy Lavender, Albert's best friends, were aboard the *Fintra*, again on the same run as the *Esneh* and *Merope*. Both sadly died when this ship was sunk.
S.S. Manchester Commerce	Albert joined the *Manchester Commerce* in February 1943 back to the United Kingdom. He remained with this vessel on its journey to Saint John, Canada. He continued back to Alexandria and other African ports before heading back across the Atlantic to New York.

Ship	Albert's History
H.M.S. Beverley & S.S. Lancastrian Prince	Both ships were sunk as part of the *Manchester Commerce* convoy to Canada, on 11 and 12 April 1943.
S.S. Hallfried	Norwegian cargo vessel which was part of a convoy Albert was in (aboard the *Manchester Commerce*). Was torpedoed and sunk in the Atlantic.
H.M.S. Saker	Albert was drafted to the shore-based *H.M.S. Saker* while he awaited his next posting, after being discharged from the *Manchester Commerce* due to illness.
S.S. Samspelga	Albert joined up with the *Samspelga* at Baltimore and journeys to New York before continuing on to Naples and Gibraltar.
S.S. Samois	One of the liberty ships supplied by the U.S.A. to aid in the war effort. Albert mentions serving on this vessel but no detail is given.
H.M.S. Flying Fox	Albert was demobbed from here, in Bristol, at the end of the War.

Printed in Great Britain
by Amazon